Prepared by the Special Publications Division
National Geographic Society
Washington, D. C.

Life in Rural America

LIFE IN RURAL AMERICA

Contributing Authors
CLAY ANDERSON, RONALD M. FISHER,
  STRATFORD C. JONES, BILL PETERSON,
  CYNTHIA RUSS RAMSAY

Published by
THE NATIONAL GEOGRAPHIC SOCIETY
MELVIN M. PAYNE, *President*
MELVILLE BELL GROSVENOR, *Editor-in-Chief*
GILBERT M. GROSVENOR, *Editor*

Prepared by
THE SPECIAL PUBLICATIONS DIVISION
ROBERT L. BREEDEN, *Editor*
DONALD J. CRUMP, *Associate Editor*
PHILIP B. SILCOTT, *Senior Editor*
MERRILL WINDSOR, *Managing Editor*
DR. OLAF F. LARSON, *Consultant, Professor
  of Rural Sociology, Cornell University*
SUSAN C. BURNS, TONI EUGENE, PATRICIA
  FRAKES, BARBARA GRAZZINI, ELIZABETH L.
  PARKER, *Research*

Illustrations
WILLIAM L. ALLEN, *Picture Editor*
SUSAN C. BURNS, RONALD M. FISHER,
  STRATFORD C. JONES, EMORY KRISTOF,
  ROBERT W. MADDEN, CYNTHIA RUSS
  RAMSAY, WENDY VAN DUYNE, *Picture Legends*

Design and Art Direction
JOSEPH A. TANEY, *Staff Art Director*
JOSEPHINE B. BOLT, *Associate Art Director*
URSULA PERRIN, *Designer*

Production and Printing
ROBERT W. MESSER, *Production Manager*
GEORGE V. WHITE, *Assistant Production
  Manager*
RAJA D. MURSHED, NANCY W. GLASER,
  Production Assistants
JOHN R. METCALFE, *Engraving and Printing*
MARY L. BERNARD, MARY G. BURNS, JANE H.
  BUXTON, MARTA ISABEL COONS, CAROL A.
  ENQUIST, SUZANNE J. JACOBSON, PENELOPE
  A. LOEFFLER, JOAN PERRY, MARILYN L.
  WILBUR, *Staff Assistants*
MARTHA K. HIGHTOWER, BRIT AABAKKEN
  PETERSON, *Index*

*Overleaf: Bareback riders Matt, Francie, and
Joe Urick head homeward from their one-room
country schoolhouse near Belt, Montana.*
*Page 1: Still a familiar rural landmark, a Texas
windmill stands idle in the late afternoon sun.*
*Endpapers: With their dog, Otto, the Urick
children explore a hill called Rocky Butte.*

OVERLEAF AND ENDPAPERS: NICHOLAS DEVORE III; PAGE 1: EPA-
DOCUMERICA, BLAIR PITTMAN; HARD-COVER DESIGN: ARLINKA BLAIR

DAVID BRILL

*At 75 the oldest competitor, Louis Skinkis
waits with his team of draft horses during
a pulling contest at Wisconsin's
Sheboygan County Fair. "I've always
used horses for my farm work," Mr.
Skinkis says. "I own a tractor but I
leave the driving to my hired help."*

Foreword

I learned early in life that rural, small-town America has a fullness and a promise. With my boyhood friends, I shared the luxurious pace of my native Danville, Kentucky, in the 1930's. We understood the inviolate rhythm of the seasons that signals the time to plant and the time to harvest, the time for football and the time for picnics. Many of those friends — and I envy them for it — still live in the town and on the surrounding farms.

The people in such places know that what the earth yields cannot — without penalty — be wrested away violently. The earth is friend also, and must be cared for and respected. The sometimes capricious elements must be accommodated.

The decades since my youth have brought their changes. The city has long been my home. But like many city dwellers, I still go wistfully to watch the rural people at the fairs. I listen to the honest music of the country. When traveling, I often turn aside from the drawing-board monotony of the interstate routes to explore the byways and to renew my spirits.

Thus, it is perhaps inevitable that as writer and photographer I frequently go home to rural America to draw upon its limitless storehouse of beauty, its lore, and its infinite truth. Always, I am welcomed and rewarded.

On one hot summer afternoon, my research for a NATIONAL GEOGRAPHIC magazine article led me to the Appalachian home of 75-year-old Loggie Renner. Loggie patiently explained to me the medicinal value of the dozens of herbs, roots, and barks the mountains provide. And he explained why his lush garden never fails. He plants it "by the signs," the stages of the moon and the position of the stars. "The moon, and the stars around it, are like a big nature's clock," he told me.

Another day, while working on my book *Stinking Creek*, I stood upon the tired, thin soil of a ridge farm with a quiet man named Gilbert Bargo. He knelt to the ground and filled his lean, cupped hands. "The earth can only stand so much," he said. Then he gently replaced the precious dirt.

In the long history of man, all of us Americans are but a moment removed from the plains, the mountains, the rivers, the farms, the villages — and from our own frontier. This book is a sampling of rural America today, in its great breadth and diversity, as seen by a team of writers and photographers. I know personally, and cherish, some of the people in these pages. Many I have not known before. But now, together, we shall meet them and visit for a time, and I am sure we shall become friends. In so doing, we rededicate ourselves to the heritage that all of us share.

JOHN FETTERMAN

Sheep moving to a hillside pasture funnel under the highway near Shell, Wyoming, as a school bus rolls by. The bus collects children along a 20-mile route and takes them to Greybull.

Contents

Morning mist rising beyond a field of corn veils a dairy farm in eastern Wisconsin. "The

Chapter One

Introduction: "Getting back to our roots"

United States," wrote American historian Richard Hofstadter, "was born in the country."

By Bill Peterson

I grew up where the prairie meets the Minnesota lake country. The earth there is black and the winters are hard. The temperature falls to 30 below zero, and the snow sometimes drifts as high as the roof of my parents' back porch. We were "town kids," but with the lake within a stone's throw, the first muskrat huts only a quarter mile away, and the first farm a quarter mile beyond, we were never far from the country.

A carpenter who works when he wants, hunts and fishes when he doesn't, still lives on one side of my parents' place; the home of a plumber, one of the town's most astute businessmen, is on the other. Long before my time, Sinclair Lewis had grown up 15 miles down U. S. Highway 52 in Sauk Centre, which was thinly disguised as Gopher Prairie in his novel *Main Street*.

We don't have a library in our town. Or a traffic light. About 1,300 people live there now, only 400 more than in 1900. Most are of Scandinavian or German descent; many are either very old or very young. Their names and faces change as the years pass. So do the places of business along Main Street; a storefront is remodeled, another is boarded up. But the pace and fabric of life continue much the same as they did decades ago: the endless conversations about the weather, the high school football games, the exodus north during duck and deer hunting seasons, the Memorial Day parade, the weekly round of coffees and civic meetings, harvest time, church services—and always, the five-month winters.

The town doesn't look like much from the interstate highway leading to "the cities," as Minneapolis and St. Paul are invariably called: just another grove clustered against the horizon, with only a water tower, the light poles on the high school athletic field, and the steeple of the Catholic church to distinguish it from the other groves that dot the rolling prairie.

The business district is compressed into three city blocks. The Empress Theater, where movies cost nine cents when I was a boy; Dick's Super Outlet; the Westside Pool Hall; the First National Bank, and Gillis Drug catch the visitor's eye. Huge elm and ash trees shade the quiet streets of modest, wood-frame homes.

Nothing earth-shattering happens there. The two things that caused the most stir in the last year, reports Robert Kremer, editor of the weekly newspaper, were a bond issue for the county hospital and a plan to build, about 30 miles away, an experimental "new town" with an eventual population of 200,000. Most people were for the bond issue but against the experimental city, he said. "There's a feeling that we live up here so we don't have to put up with crowds."

Yet life is busy. The air is clean, the lake is inviting, the atmosphere is friendly and easygoing. People are individuals, their personalities, joys, and pains known to others. Concerns are fundamental. The sky is read as much as the afternoon newspaper. Birth is a much-discussed event. Death is front-page news, and accepted as a community tragedy.

"Here a person is somebody," one longtime resident told me.

I mention all this because, like anyone else who has lived in rural America, I can't talk about it without reference to where I knew it best. In my case, it is a little town in central Minnesota with the Indian name Osakis (pronounced O-*say*-kiss).

My nostalgia is personal, but I think it reflects a yearning embedded in even the most confirmed city dweller: a desire to return to a simpler, less hectic time, which for better or worse is most likely to be found in our small towns and countryside. In part, of course, it is a rejection of what urbanization has wrought. Despite our technology, our gadgets, our comfortable offices and all the conveniences of city living, we are dissatisfied. We long for more basic pleasures: pure air to breathe, a night sky full of stars, the satisfaction of work done with our own hands — perhaps in the rich earth itself — a sense of place, and passers-by on the street who smile and ask, "How you doin' today?" And we feel — perhaps mistakenly sometimes — that we can find these things in rural America.

Ed Pollard is convinced that he did. A sturdy, ruddy-faced man in his early forties, he is the Osakis fire chief, a former mayor, and the operator of Pollard's Mill and Elevator Company.

Once he wanted to become a chemist. "But then hunting season came along," he said, "and I started thinking, you can't hardly beat the life around here. So I packed my bags and came home from college to go hunting. I never did finish school.

"No, never regretted it," he continued, looking thoroughly content in his office, a small, dusty alcove behind his sales counter. "Any afternoon I can take off and play a round of golf or go fishing and no one can hassle me about it."

Pollard spends much of his spare time on civic affairs. Yet he isn't the unabashed small-town booster one might imagine. "There's a shortage of people to do things, a lack of leadership in places like this," he said. "Membership of the church boards, the city council, and the school board doesn't change often enough. The town suffers from stagnation and complacency."

Religion and an attachment to the land run deep in the surrounding countryside. One Saturday my father and I stopped at Roy Larson's place northeast of town in an area called "Snoose Valley" (for the snuff used by the Norwegian Lutherans who first settled there). Larson created a minor furor a few years back when he built a $60,000 dairy barn and covered the floors of the stalls with indoor-outdoor carpeting. He is a well-educated, deeply religious man with a reputation as a top dairy farmer. To my surprise he said he once studied for the ministry. "But then Roy felt a calling to farm," Esther Larson explained. "The Lord charts a lot of different paths for His followers."

No one is very rich in our town. The Lutheran parsonage is one of the most expensive homes. There are only four small factories, and limited employment opportunities. When you ask people why they live there, they say, "Everybody here is as good as everybody else," or "It's a great place to raise kids."

The last time I visited, it was midsummer. The waters of Lake Osakis were sky blue, the yards were a lush green, nights were

LOWELL GEORGIA (BELOW AND OPPOSITE, BELOW)

Skirts swirl to the call of "curlique" during a club square dance at Krazy Korner, a renovated Army barracks in Buena Vista, Georgia. Records rather than live musicians now provide the music at most country square dances. But fiddlers still shine at such events as the centennial celebration in David City, Nebraska, where farmer Fritz Struebing strikes up a hoedown tune. About 55 years ago he swapped his bicycle for the violin he still plays; he took lessons in classical music but picked up "fiddlin' " on his own. At right, good humor speeds a long day's work for Mrs. Tillie Tschetter (with spoon) and Mrs. Elizabeth Hofer as they bone 475 pounds of stewing beef for the annual Schmeckfest or "tasting festival" in Freeman, South Dakota, sponsored by the area's Mennonites.

refreshingly cool. But I was discouraged to find that two more stores had closed, and the town hadn't recruited a new doctor since Doc Emerson—E. E. Emerson, M.D.—closed his practice.

Newman Olson, whom we called "Tuky" before he became president of the First National Bank, thinks the town is "essentially over the hump" after some hard times. The flight from the farms has leveled off, he told me. Lakeshore prices are soaring. Retired people are clamoring for homes. And—for the first time in decades—a few young people are moving back.

"People want to get out of the cities," he said. "It's the old case of wanting to get back to their roots."

What are our roots? What attracts people to rural America?

I'm not sure. But my grandfather Ray S. Brooks, who has been close to the soil all his life and broke a wild horse on his 80th birthday, gave one answer I like: "I just want to live where I can stretch my arms without hitting someone else in the face."

His father settled in Dakota Territory when houses were still made of sod. In those days—as has been the case for most of our history—we were a rural people. As late as 1880, only 28.2 percent of our population lived in cities of more than 2,500. At the close of the century Woodrow Wilson could say, "The history of a nation is only the history of its villages written large."

That is no longer true. The Commission on Population Growth estimates that 85 percent of all Americans will live in metropolitan areas by the year 2000. We have become a nation of congested cities, smelly factories, sprawling suburbs, neon lights, and impersonal office buildings, connected from one coast to the other by airline routes and concrete highways in a vast montage of sameness.

We can travel for thousands of miles and miss the pulse of the heartland: the diversity of the wheat farmer, tobacco grower, and small-town druggist. At highway speeds we can still appreciate the immensity and beauty of the Arizona desert or the lushness of the Illinois cornfields; but unless we leave the sterile interstate ribbons for the back roads of America, we miss the stern propriety of New England, the grace and amenity of the South, the quiet strength of the mountain country, and the matter-of-fact optimism of the West.

We miss the people.

Looking crisp and unruffled, W. W. (Bill) Godfrey stood on a low platform in the entryway of a red barn near Lyme, New Hampshire. "What-a-ya give for a gen-u-ine brass clock?" he was saying in the rat-a-tat-tat voice of an experienced auctioneer. "What-a-ya give for the clock? It'll run when you do. It'll run as long as you do. And it'll stop when you stop. What-a-ya give?"

The afternoon was hot for New England—about 94°—but the crowd at the Bolea Farm was still large after four hours. "Auctions are some of the biggest social events we have 'round here," one man explained. But car license plates from New York, Massachusetts, and Pennsylvania indicated the interest was more than local.

By profession Godfrey is a mortician. At 74 he says, "There is hardly anyone I knew in this village in the old days that I haven't auctioned off or buried."

His style is a homespun, humorous one, developed in five decades of auctioneering. A short, slightly built man, he looks younger than his years. On this occasion he wore a straw hat, bow tie, white shirt, and blue suspenders. His eyes twinkled engagingly.

"And here we have an Atwater Kent radio," he declared, exhibiting a set of about 1925 vintage. "Guaranteed not to keep you awake. Not a screech left in it. What-a-ya give for this fine radio?"

A young man in a T-shirt nodded his head.

"Two dollars. Do I hear four? I hear four. Do I hear five? The man over here says ten. Do I hear twelve?"

The bidding crept upward, eventually pitting a crusty-looking antique dealer against a young woman. It stopped at $27.50.

"And sold to the lady in red for twenty-seven and a half," Godfrey declared. "Sold to the lady who wants to miss the news."

Though I doubt that the woman bought the broken radio in order to miss the news, thousands of people have swarmed into New England and other rural areas during the last decade seeking calm and quiet. Many came only to visit, or to look for antiques and other mementos of a simpler life. But thousands bought land: some for permanent residences; many for second homes, giving Vermont a "shadow population" almost as large as its permanent population of 443,000.

Bill Godfrey watches both the newcomers and the reaction they've caused with bemusement. Auction prices, he says, have skyrocketed. "Some of these people must be nutty or they'd never buy some of the things we sell," he told me at his home on Blood Brook Road in Ely, Vermont. "Why, last year, a bunch was wanting to buy three-hole outhouse seats. If I had filled my house and barn with junk that people were giving away a few years back, I could be a millionaire now."

Unlike some old-timers, Godfrey doesn't mind the newcomers. "A few years ago the state set up a program to get folks to move in here. Now that they talked them into it, they turn right around and try to discourage folks from coming. It doesn't make sense to me. Besides," he added, "a lot of good folks moved in."

That evening I found myself with a family of newcomers, the Hardings, who had known city living in Washington, Chicago, and Louisville and found it wanting.

"In urban or suburban society, there are a lot of hidden pressures. You get sucked into them without realizing it. There's just too much of everything—too much to do, too much expected," Gordon Harding was saying after a lazy supper that lasted until dusk. His wife, Judy, gregarious and open-faced, sat beside him.

Harding, a compact man in his late thirties, had been a highly regarded newspaper picture editor living in a fashionable suburb when I last saw him. Now, a year later, he had a new career as an automobile mechanic and a new life halfway up a small mountain three miles south of Randolph Center, Vermont (population 140).

New England newcomer Gordon Harding repairs a Volkswagen crankcase in his shop near Randolph Center, Vermont. In 1972 he left a newspaper career as a photographer-editor and moved to the country with his wife, Judy, and their four daughters, seeking a simpler life. "It reached the point that there were too many middlemen—in my job as well as in our daily lives," says Harding. "Here we rely more on ourselves."

WILLIAM L. ALLEN, NATIONAL GEOGRAPHIC STAFF

With his short, sandy brown hair and easygoing manner, he isn't the embittered social dropout. He is simply seeking a better life for himself and his family.

The year had its bumpy times. Harding had decided he could afford to go without income long enough to build a five-bedroom house and auto repair shop on his 4½ acres of land. He thought it would take six months. It took eight, and even then he hadn't really finished. The snow came, and the family learned that weather in rural New England can't be ignored as they had ignored it in the city. Here driveways had to be plowed, ice scraped from the roof, overshoes bought for six people.

By fall of the second year, business at Harding's Center Garage would be booming. But it started slowly, and money ran short. Work stopped on the huge house with its gambrel roof. Floors remained uncovered; walls went without plaster or wallboard.

But the Hardings found contentment. "Try building a house with your own hands," Gordon said. "Drive every nail, cut every board, nail every shingle. Be both plumber and electrician. That is getting down to basics. And it's mighty rewarding."

We walked outside to my car. We could see Harding's repair shop 150 yards down the slope. The night was clear, and the stars illuminated the unspoiled valley.

I recalled what Judy, a Chicago native, had said a few minutes before: "We've learned a lot about ourselves here. We've found we're not suburbanites. Deep down, we're country people."

In her town on the windswept South Dakota prairie, Mrs. Harriet Larson longs for newcomers. "The trouble is, there's nothing to hold the young people," she explained one dusty day in late summer. "There are no jobs, no opportunities, and now even the school is closed down."

Prim and soft-spoken, Mrs. Larson is a native of Garden City. For 34 years she has been postmaster there. "Garden City has never been a really big place," she said. "Once it was between 300 and 400. But now we're down to about a hundred people."

Memories of a more glorious past linger amid the decay. Weeds grow around the empty red-brick school house; homes stand vacant, dust clinging to the faded paint. The hotel is gone, and so is the windmill that for decades pumped the water supply. The harness racetrack at the edge of town is deserted. The only restaurant is closed. Wein's Grocery has been converted into a lodge hall. Nerger's General Store, which my grandfather A. M. Peterson managed during the Depression, has become a potato warehouse.

Only a branch bank, a farm implement store, a service station, the grain elevator, the post office, and KDLO, a television transmitting station on the outskirts of town, survive. "Biggest crowds we ever had here came when they put up that TV tower," Mrs. Larson recalled. "People came to watch from miles around."

Years later the station still attracts an occasional curious visitor, she added, gazing absentmindedly out the post office window across the empty street. "People assume that any place that has a television station can't be too small."

At the Standard Oil station a few doors away, Mrs. Emogene Lawrence sighed, "We're all just hanging on here."

Such admissions come hard. But the sad fact is that Garden City and dozens of the very small towns on the midwestern plains are dying. Once the pride of the surrounding farm country, many of them sprang up less than a century ago as the railroads opened up the prairie. They thrived as commercial centers until the droughts and Depression of the 1930's, and some until after World War II. But in recent years the farms that supported them have been caught in a vicious cycle of staggering machinery costs, fluctuating prices, and low profit margins. As operations were consolidated for greater efficiency, the farms grew larger and fewer.

Statistics from the Census Bureau and the Department of Agriculture tell part of the story. They show that the 15.6 million Americans living on farms in 1960 had been reduced to 9.7 million in 1970. South Dakota was especially hard hit; while much of the nation grew steadily during the 1960's, that state lost 2.2 percent of its population, mostly from rural areas.

In Garden City, John Grout, a slender-shouldered man with a domelike bald head, stubbornly holds out at his market across the street from the Farmers and Merchants Bank. "I'm 72 years old, and I've been threatening to quit," he declared. "But I'll stay as long as I can make a living and a little on the side."

Two customers entered as he spoke. He greeted both by their first names. They collected a few items and said, "Charge it, John." In the age of impersonal supermarkets, Grout's grocery is a throwback to the neighborhood store. It is a gathering hall, a community social center.

That's the way Grout thinks things should be. "I like to live in a town where I'm called by my first name," he explained. His own sons left Garden City long ago for larger places, and he harbors no hope that they'll ever move back. But he deeply resents anyone who looks down his nose at this town.

"We're not backwoods hicks here," he told me. "We're intelligent people, just as intelligent as anyone in Washington, D. C., or any other city. The way things look, maybe more so."

Many of the old clichés about rural America don't apply anymore. The lines between rural and urban life, between "country bumpkin and city slicker," have faded with education, television, high-speed highways, and air travel. Many present-day rural dwellers have lived in cities, or make frequent visits there; others are suburbanites simply living a little farther out.

"We could live and work anyplace, but this is where we wanted to be," Lewis Veghte, Jr., told me one afternoon at his restored early 19th-century farmhouse near Piermont, New Hampshire.

Ten years ago Veghte gave up a job as a Congressional aide to move from the national capital to rural New England. He had learned to love the area while a student at Dartmouth in nearby Hanover, but there was more involved in the move than that.

"I had come to the conclusion that privacy is a very important facet of good living," he explained. "The type of life we have here is what many people are really looking for."

A real estate agent living on a former dairy farm tucked into the New Hampshire hills, Veghte has found his life drastically altered. His tractor, fields, and woods replaced tennis and golf as his chief leisure-time interests. "Having a piece of land affects a man," he said. "He watches every little change—in the weather, in the seasons. And he learns to be himself."

When John Chalmers, a former high school classmate of mine, announced to the world that he was going to work as a hired farmhand, everyone thought he was crazy. It was 1964, he had just graduated from the University of Illinois, and he had a young bride and a lucrative job offer from a Chicago bank.

"Instead, I went to work on a farm for $200 a month," he recalled. "Like I said, people thought I was an idiot."

Why did he do it?

"I don't know," he said. Dusk had fallen, and we were leaning against a fence in his backyard. The stench of pig manure permeated the air. An August moon rose on the horizon.

"I suppose I wanted to prove something. They said a guy couldn't make it starting from scratch."

Chalmers has—in a hurry. At a time when the average age of farm operators in the United States is 51, he is 31. He didn't grow up on a farm, and he had no land-rich relative to stake him when he went deep into debt to buy his own place in 1969. Only 40 acres, it is dwarfed by the surrounding farms with their vast cornfields. Yet in 1972 his hog operation grossed more than $200,000, putting it among the top 2 percent of the nation's farms in terms of gross receipts.

Chalmers likes the wholesomeness and independence of farm life. But he regards many farmers as old-fashioned, handicapped by their own backgrounds and by conservative small-town banks. "The traditional farmer," he said as we inspected some of the 9,000 hogs he would market during the year, "had three ideals: hard work, long hours, and being debt free. The young, modern farm manager works just as hard, but if he can borrow $7,000 to make $20,000, he'll sure do it.

"I don't care what business you're in: You either have to get more and more efficient or increase your volume to make more money."

The Chalmers place is located at the end of a winding, oiled road outside Oakford, Illinois. It looks more like a factory than a farm. There is no majestic red barn. Instead, the hogs are housed in four new corrugated-metal buildings that, on the outside, look like warehouses. Inside, the environment is carefully controlled. Sows are placed in individual stalls two or three days before they're ready to give birth. Their piglets then remain confined in one of the buildings for the rest of their time on the farm, simply being shifted from one small pen to another as they grow older. Their feed is mixed in a miniature processing plant that adjoins the complex, then is carried to storage bins through pneumatic tubes. The stalls are washed down with high-pressure hoses.

Chalmers designed and helped build the complex himself. "A hog farmer has to be a little of everything—plumber, electrician, veterinarian, chemist, businessman," he said later that night in the kitchen. His wife, Linda, mother of two, nodded in agreement. She was blonde and stylish in her blue outfit. He was short and intense, his curly brown hair cropped close to his head. His waist was firm. He noticed mine wasn't. "On a farm you have a chance to develop your management skills and build your muscles, too," he said. "It's good for a man; keeps him from getting soft."

R. A. Patterson certainly hasn't gotten soft, I thought a few days later as the red pickup in which I was riding bounded down the roadway. Pat and I were delivering horse feed to one of his customers near the southern edge of Arizona's scenic Oak Creek Canyon. But Pat's mind was on ranching. "I don't classify myself as one of the better cattle ranchers around. But I enjoy it—it's a challenge to me," he said. "Now my brother-in-law—I consider him one of the top cattlemen in the state."

Patterson, 49, is a part-time rancher who'd like to work at it full time. Tall and husky, he has an arresting gentleness in his voice. His ancestors were among the first Mormons to cross the arid West. He continues the traditions of their faith, serving as an officer in the Church of Jesus Christ of Latter-day Saints and encouraging his seven children to fulfill two-year, unpaid missionary assignments in such faraway places as Paraguay and Germany. His wife, Eudora, is a fourth-generation cattlewoman, and loves the life. "A ranch is a beautiful family tie," she says. "It brings us together."

The Pattersons live in Cottonwood, a trading center for Verde Valley farmers and ranchers. *(Continued on page 24)*

Called from play, Daisy Yoder stands resignedly as her mother fastens her head scarf against the chill. Their home-sewn clothing, of a style adapted from 18th-century rural European dress, reflects the simple life of Old Order Amish, a religious sect whose members decline to use most modern conveniences. Built in the 1870's, the Yoder farmhouse near Gortner in western Maryland's Pleasant Valley has been expanded and remodeled but has no electricity or telephone. On the porch, a pump stands atop the century-old, hand-dug well that still supplies the family's water. Change comes slowly to the Amish. They prudently adopt only innovations they think will not disturb community harmony or conflict with their strict religious beliefs.

Amid a clutter of wares in his store, Jefferson Blair mends shoes on a treadle sewing machine. A sign outside reads, "Let us repair your shoes sell you grocerys donut flour mix, also receipe comes with the flour and do mechinest work sell fishing tackels fish bate hrdware." The store in Dyer, Kentucky—population 60— stocks everything from tricycles and corn pads to hair rollers and casket handles. Below, Jeff and his wife, Lena, sit on one of the benches where townspeople gather to talk or to read their mail. The store also serves as Dyer's post office; the Blairs' daughter, Shirley, is postmaster. A sign directs customers to the after-hours mail slot; those without stamps drop in money for postage with their letters.

Pat runs a feed store there, and with his brother-in-law, State Senator Boyd Tenney, owns a ranch at Hackberry in the dry, high juniper country of Mohave County, a rugged four-hour drive from Cottonwood. The ranch house has no electricity, telephone, doorbell, television, or nosy neighbors.

"When I go up there I won't even allow a radio or clock in the place," said Eudora Patterson. "We have to take a calendar so we know when to come home."

Pat spends several weeks a year at the ranch—branding cattle, rounding them up for sale, developing new water supplies, checking for disease and for coyotes that might disturb the herd. Often relatives and friends join in.

"It's nothing to bed down 50 people in the front room and bunkhouse," Mrs. Patterson said. "The women cook. All the men and boys work like dogs. They get up, saddle their horses, and wait for daybreak. When it gets dark they say, 'We've still got another good hour,' and keep going. Our kids have learned what real work is."

We had spent three hours delivering sacks of feed and bales of hay to well-to-do horse owners in the red butte and mesa country around Sedona. Now the pickup headed toward Cottonwood past more new homes, shops, art galleries, and real estate offices.

"When I came to this country after the war, this was all cattle range," Pat said. "There wasn't a thing here. You could buy all the land you wanted for $125 an acre."

He paused, reflecting, then added:

"To tell the truth, I wish it would have stayed small. Back then, people pulled together. We've always had clean air, an ideal climate, water. I hate to see it spoiled."

The land of California's San Joaquin Valley is flat, rich, and dry. In summer the days begin hot and stay hot, especially in the fields where the farm workers toil, their faces drawn taut by the sun, their backs worn weary by years of labor. Eugenio Lopez is one of them. By 6:30 each weekday morning he arrives at one of the grape fields or citrus groves near Delano. He will stay there for at least nine hours, trying to earn enough money to support his wife and six children.

By farm-worker standards, he does well for them. After 17 years in the vineyards, he is skilled in the ways of the grapes. Table grapes require more attention than most crops; they must be sprayed, trimmed, and thinned as well as picked—all jobs that Lopez does well. The process extends over ten months, enabling him to live year around in Delano, heart of the table-grape country. The work, Lopez says, is hard but "muy bueno." His wages have increased from 70 cents an hour to $2.60 in union fields, and growers have been required to provide rest rooms and give coffee breaks.

Still, problems persist: Inflation seems to eat up wage increases, strikes may idle fields, and there are times of the year when work is scarce, when Lopez has to look hard for a day's work.

"No, no, the money is never sufficient," he said as we sat in his spare but tidy home. His wife, Matilda, a polite, round-faced

In a cafe in Edom, Texas, rancher Ruby Lee Miller pauses to greet artisans Sharon and Doug Brown, who moved to the town in 1971. Outside his pottery studio, Doug trims a vase with Sharon's help. The studio and the Browns' adjoining silversmith and weaving shops serve as a center for Edom's growing group of craftsmen.

woman, radiated a gentle strength. Her husband, small, wiry, and ramrod straight, is one of America's restless working poor.

I have encountered many such men, scarred by poverty and despair, in the coal camps of Appalachia and on the tenant farms of the South. They are the people left behind in our society's march toward the good life. Many—crippled by age, lack of education, illness, and defeat—have given up. A few have hope. The Lopezes are among them.

Both were born in Mexico and came to the California grape and citrus fields because there was not enough work in their homeland. They still speak little English, read even less. But they are proud people who want no pity; proud parents who want to rear their children in the best way possible. They live in a four-room duplex in a public housing project. I spent several hours there, with the Lopezes' second oldest son, David, serving as interpreter. I was impressed with the closeness of the family and their hopes for the youngsters. "After school finishes," David said, "my parents want me and my brothers and sisters to go to college."

But the obstacles are great for the Lopez children and thousands like them at the bottom of the economic ladder in rural America— where a third of the nation's poverty and more than half of its substandard housing are found, and where health and education services are often inadequate.

The history of the California farm worker has been one of exploitation and human tragedy since the early Spaniards began using Indians almost as slaves. Later landholders looking for a cheap labor supply hired former Chinese railroad workers; the Chinese were succeeded by Japanese, and the Japanese by Asian Indians, Mexicans, and Filipinos. Then the Mexicans were displaced to make room for hungry Okies, Arkies, and Texans in the 1930's—the Depression and Dust Bowl days of John Steinbeck's

The Grapes of Wrath—only to be urged to return a few years later. Always, wages remained low and working conditions deplorable.

Often migratory, made hesitant by illiteracy and indebtedness, intimidated by growers' opposition, the farm workers failed until recent years to organize effectively. Even so, blood was spilled—as long ago as 1913, when a district attorney, a deputy sheriff, and two workers were killed in a riot, and then in a series of other incidents over six decades. Ironically, recent violence grew out of conflict between two unions—the United Farm Workers and the International Brotherhood of Teamsters—and a new cohesion between growers and the Teamsters.

When I visited Lopez, bloodshed had returned to the valley. Death had claimed two farm workers within the week. One died from injuries received while being arrested; the other was shot while on picket duty. They were buried as martyrs by the UFW, and thousands of mourners marched in the funeral processions carrying the black-eagle flag of the union.

Lopez supports the UFW's Cesar Chavez, describing him as the first labor leader to help farm workers raise their standard of living. But tensions run high. Our path led to a neighboring house where a woman was alone with her two children. My presence obviously made her uneasy. The deaths had frightened her, and she feared for her husband's safety. Her speech was guarded and hesitant. Finally she said, "I don't have confidence in anyone anymore. I don't trust anybody. Too much has happened here."

Hardship and turmoil have too often been part of the life of rural Americans, contributing to a fatalistic view of life that is reflected in much country music. In Ivydale, West Virginia, the hills and the hard times have produced a musical style with a special old-time flavor. "Music is all over this neighborhood," John Morris said to me one Saturday on his front porch. "I couldn't have missed it if I tried."

John, now 27, started early. He was just six when his grandfather Amos Morris taught him to play "Cripple Creek" on the family banjo. By the time he was a teen-ager he was playing the fiddle and the guitar, and had started making banjos of his own from walnut, ebony, and parts of old Buick transmissions.

He grew up in an age of rock music and electric guitars, but they never attracted him like the old-fashioned fiddlers and banjo players in his neighborhood. "The old-time music is something to identify with," he said. "It's part of our mountain culture."

John, fiercely independent but quiet of speech, hopes to preserve this heritage. When he finished college and his brother, David, returned from a tour of duty in Viet Nam, they decided to stake out a career as professional folk singers and musicians. They have organized mountain folk festivals for the Rockefeller Foundation and they play college campuses, parties, theaters—"wherever they'll have us." The high point of their year, however, remains the Morris Family Old-Time Music Festival, an event that attracts 5,000 lovers of old-time music.

The Morris brothers gather their material and the musicians for their festivals from the hills and hollows of Clay County, West Virginia, and the rest of Appalachia. "We just sort of take old songs, mostly from people 'round here," John explained. "It's traditional material, strictly old-time stuff."

He paused, tuning his sassafras fiddle. It had rained during the night, and the air was damp and cool. Just then Gruder Morris and his wife, Jennie, drove past in their pickup. "You come over here," John yelled toward the road. "We'll have us some music."

Gruder screeched his pickup to a halt, threw it into reverse, and wheeled into the driveway. He emerged from the truck with a banjo in one hand.

"Let's play us a little music to watch the wind go by," John said.

Gruder nodded. He is an old friend and distant cousin of the Morris brothers as well as a fine musician. For years he delivered mail by horseback in the Ivydale area. But this day he was only interested in music. He settled in a corner of the concrete porch, picking his banjo. John joined him, playing slowly at first, gradually increasing the tempo: "Cripple Creek," "Arkansas Traveler," "Minnow on the Hook," "Sally Ann," and "The Wreck of Old 97."

Gruder's wife; John's wife, Deloris; his father, Dallis, a schoolteacher; and 2½-year-old John Amos Morris gathered as the music spilled into the morning. There were many approving smiles and much tapping of feet. Both musicians enjoyed the attention, but pointed out that such sessions are almost everyday occurrences.

After a brief rest they were back at it, playing old mountain song after song for almost two hours. When I left, Gruder was still picking at his banjo. "Oh, I could stay here all day and play," he said. "Go without dinner and not even miss it."

The sun dropped even with the treetops as the Class of 1973 marched in single file across Colee Field in Magnolia, Mississippi. Clad in blue-gray robes, half the class started under each goal post and the two files met at the 50-yard line. The strains of "Pomp and Circumstance," traditional hymn of spring, swelled in the background. A white banner proclaimed: "He Conquers, Who Conquers Himself."

The Class of '73, everyone agreed, was truly a remarkable one. The girls' basketball team had won the Amateur Athletic Union national championship; the boys had finished second in the Mississippi South State tournament.

But even more important, the class had survived racial desegregation, the social revolution that swept this part of the South in the late 1960's and divided many communities—including Magnolia—with tension and distrust. Some whites transferred their children to private academies, and some blacks complained of continuing racism. But the transition was accomplished. "We've been through some times when very little education took place," confessed Superintendent Herbert S. Hoff. "No one was really satisfied. But we've accepted it and moved along."

Now an audience of almost a thousand, black and white,

gathered in the high school stadium. "A few years ago a ceremony like this would have been real tense," said Allen L. Coney, an administrator in Pike County's Negro schools for 34 years and now assistant superintendent of the integrated district. "Tonight you won't find anything unusual."

I had decided to visit the ceremony because I knew high school graduation is the great divide, the point where old friends part and new careers start, the time in much of rural America when the mass departure for the city begins.

Not so many years ago, most of the graduating class from Eva Gordon High, Magnolia's old black school, would head north immediately after graduation, a few catching the first Illinois Central train or Greyhound bus out of town. "In the next two weeks you couldn't find a single member of the class left around here," said Eugene Patterson, a black guidance counselor. Many of the whites weren't far behind.

That is changing, Patterson said. More than a third of the graduates now go to college, most in Mississippi. Others find jobs in several new factories that have opened up near town.

Still, the divide continues. By graduation day 1973, five or six senior girls had announced their intention to marry before the end of summer; Keith McCrimon, president of the student body at one of the school's two campuses, and half a dozen other boys had volunteered for the armed services; and others like Lana Marie Ball, star of the girl's basketball team, knew things would never be the same again. Lana planned to go to college in the fall and eventually become a teacher, but she admitted, "My days in the limelight are over.

"This graduation is real important to me," she said a few minutes before the ceremonies were to begin. "It means I'll have to make a lot of decisions on my own from now on."

Tall and slender, with high cheekbones, she adjusted her mortarboard over her long, sandy hair. "Still, I'm not very excited about it," she added. "Kind of sad, really."

The ceremony was short and simple. There was no outside speaker. Instead, two graduates addressed the class: valedictorian Kaye Francis Alford, a white, and Linda Ann Williams, a black, who intends to study pharmacy at the University of Mississippi.

Linda chose "Happy Birthday, America" as her topic because, she said, "We should never give up on our country." Her voice, unsteady at first, soon gathered volume and confidence. "Our problem today isn't so much the noise of the bad," she said. "It's the silence of the good. Let's not let the historians write, 'This nation died because no one cared.'"

Kaye spoke more sternly. "The cry of my generation has been, and continues to be, 'Give us more freedom,'" she declared. "We have flung off one restraint after another, only to find that we have not learned to restrain ourselves.

"But one day the good teen-ager will awake," she continued, "and demand the return to the principle that freedom means responsibility."

As Yazoo River waters rise, James Mann boards up a house in Eagle Lake, Mississippi, to keep out debris. In 1973 storms flooded millions of acres of farmland in the Mississippi-Missouri River Valley.

Then the 123 members of the Class of 1973 rose from their seats and walked to the podium, past the ferns and pink carnations, each to receive a handshake and a diploma from Dr. Harry C. Frye, Jr., president of the board of trustees. Bishop Donald Smith offered the benediction: "Lord, we pray Thou will go with them as they take many roads. . . . Shower Thy richest blessings upon them." At the end there were a few tears, and many proud parental smiles.

But what would happen to the Class of '73 from Magnolia, Mississippi, and a thousand other little towns in rural America? Would it follow the preceding generation into the cities to seek jobs, opportunity, happiness? Or would it find its opportunities in our small towns and countryside?

I don't know.

Jerry Tate had already made up his mind. His brother was waiting for him when the ceremony ended. They were heading for Fort Worth, Texas.

"I won't be back unless I have to," he said. "I'm just tired of it 'round here, I guess. I want to go out and try a new life."

Jerry is the youngest of eight children in a family descended from plantation slaves. School was hard for him, and graduation was the proudest moment of his young life. He wasn't sure what things would be like in Fort Worth, and he didn't like the idea of leaving Marie Reynolds, who stood dejectedly at his side.

"My brother has talked to his boss, and he says I can get a job at the General Motors plant," he said. "My brother, he's doing pretty good. He's got himself a new car and a nice brick house."

Randy Smith, senior class president, was staying.

"I love Mississippi and the South," he declared. "I've lived here 18 years, and I'm not leaving. My parents own a grocery store over in Fernwood. It's a small community—real quiet. I'll go to college, and after a few years take over the business.

"To me, it looks like a good future. A good life."

Music of Appalachia resounds from Lee (Poppy) Triplett's fiddle as he joins Dwight Diller on the banjo and John Morris on the guitar at the annual Roane-Calhoun Old-Time Music Festival in Chloe, West Virginia. Outside the Morris home, young John Amos tries to pick a rhythm on a small banjo as his father offers encouragement. Above at right, J. F. (Doc) White, 85, keeps in practice in his Ivydale office. "I used to win the blue ribbon every time, before I got arthritis," he says. Morris confirms, "He's one of the best I ever heard."

Freed of its harness, a horse grazes a lush expanse of orchard grass in Pleasant Valley, Maryland. The Amish folk who settled here in the mid-19th century still live principally by farming the rich soil.

After a ten-hour day in the fields hoeing cotton, Mrs. Lucille Tenzy attends an adult reading class in Rosedale, Mississippi. Teacher Fredericka Taylor says her students have "plenty of motivation. They want better jobs or higher self-esteem." Above, boys in Jones Village play an impromptu basketball game on a makeshift court. In Cleveland, Mississippi, travelers board a bus, some perhaps headed for a new life in a far-off city.

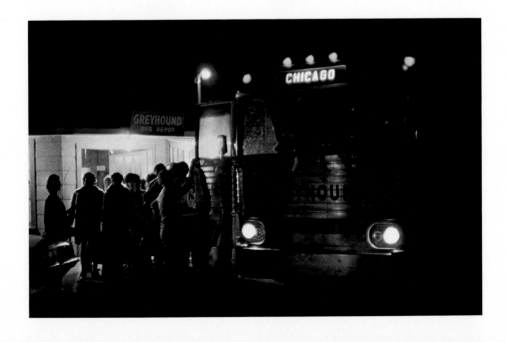

Day recedes from Monhegan Island, Maine, home of sea-hardened lobstermen and a summer

Chapter Two

Small towns:
"Here I can leave a footprint"

haven for vacationists. In winter the 65 year-round residents face fierce storms and numbing cold.

"I can do anything except bootleg and preach," said Buddy Steward, and I believed him. The evidence lay all around us as we stood in his workshop, a fascinating clutter of tools, gadgets, and pieces of machinery. "That's a Model-T Ford hubcap," he explained, pausing to glance at the object in my hand as he poked through a drawer crammed with bolts of every variety. "Someday I might find a use for it." His lean face creased in a smile remarkably impish for his 53 years.

Buddy sharpens a few saws, hones an occasional knife on a grinder driven by an old washing machine motor, and patches up furniture that is falling apart. Unless his arthritis is bothering him he is a happy man, who has never wanted to leave his hometown of Buena Vista, Georgia. "I've grown up and grown old with these people," he said. "They know me, and I know them."

I had come to Buena Vista (pronounced *Bew*-na Vista)—a community of 1,400 where people still swap stories at the post office and get together at potluck suppers—as part of a cross-country journey to learn how Americans live in small towns in the 1970's. I went to communities small enough to be considered rural, to places with a population of less than 2,500. I was curious to compare the life-style and traditions of rural Americans with my own big-city experiences.

For a look at a more isolated town, I had gone far north to Seldovia, Alaska. From the cold, choppy waters of Cook Inlet comes an abundant harvest of crab, herring, halibut, and salmon that has brought prosperity to this village of snug houses, mobile homes, unpaved lanes, and hovering mountains.

In Nevada I sped across sagebrush desert to the mining community of Gabbs, where an open-pit mine and a processing plant keep 250 people on the payroll and support a town of 850.

My path also led to the rolling hills of southeastern Indiana, where I turned off U. S. 50 to reach Milan (pronounced *My*-lun), a former fuel and water stop on the Baltimore and Ohio Railroad.

Another day, when the sap of sugar maples dripped into pails and patches of melting snow dappled the ground, I drove the back roads of Massachusetts past white, steepled churches and clapboard houses on my way to a New England town meeting.

And finally I traveled south to Buena Vista, whose shade trees and big yards taper away to cotton fields, peanut farms, and piney woods just beyond the city limits. Built around a square framing the county courthouse, the town has a turn-of-the-century look, with scant traffic and quiet streets.

"The wealth of the county was invested in slaves, land, and livestock," reads the *History of Marion County, Georgia,* which I scanned in the elegant, high-ceilinged parlor of Mrs. Robert Putnam Stevens, widow of a prominent businessman and civic leader.

With its silk-covered walls, muted brocades, and gleaming mahogany and crystal, the room recalled a bygone era when ladies led unhurried lives and their households were staffed with servants. For almost a century after the Civil War, the leisurely way of life of Buena Vista's aristocracy lingered on, based in part on a ready supply of cheap labor. But by the 1950's, increasing numbers of black workers were seeking jobs in the cities, and that trend has continued.

"Last year I couldn't get anybody to paint the garage," said the silver-haired Mrs. Stevens, at 74 still known to all as Miss Esther. "I finally said to Lightning Swanson, 'Let's you and I do the job.' But he said, 'I don't climb no ladders. I gets dizzy-headed.'"

Miss Esther's hand fluttered to the green ribbon in her hair as she spoke in the slow, soft accent of the South. "So I put on my fishing clothes and painted, while Lightning held the ladder.

"It's a lot different from what it used to be."

Jonathan Thaddeus Davis, the oldest living resident of Buena Vista, would agree. "Even 25 years ago you couldn't have made me believe there wouldn't be a single mule farm left in Marion County," he told me as he rocked slowly back and forth. "Now my grandson has two tractors and not a hired hand on the place.

"I started farming as a young boy, dropping peas and picking cotton. Dad raised us to work. Later I hoed peanuts and pulled corn, and I believe I cut about as much wood as anyone ever cut."

Uncle John sold his farm at 76 and soon retired to "a soft life in town. Now my daughter Reba, here, won't let me do a thing. If I do anything, she says I do it wrong."

These days Uncle John—who turned 101 on February 14, 1974—takes it easy. He spends much of the time on the porch of his daughter's white frame house or in the small pecan grove beyond the garden. If the weather is good, he strolls up the street to visit his friend Luther Lewis Johnson. "He's 85, but he can't get around as well as me. Sometimes we talk; sometimes we don't say a word. But we're together," Uncle John said.

In the city, age often isolates the elderly, leaving them alone and unwanted. They pine away in rest homes or spend their days in dreary apartments, unable or unwilling to venture forth. In Buena Vista, Uncle John lives out his years among relatives and friends. The whole town celebrated his hundredth birthday—twice: once in church and once in the town hall. And there is always someone to listen to him reminisce about old times.

"A candy pulling—now, that was something. First the cane syrup cooked with water and vinegar till it got to candy. We young folks would butter our hands and get us a wad. Then, with a gal partner, we'd pull and pull that candy. Oh, we used to have the biggest kind of time that way."

John Davis can't see much now, for cataracts blur both eyes. But his mind is sharp, his appetite is hearty, and his spirits are high. He explained his long life as "the Lord's doing. And I was always pretty slow and lazy. I reckon that part helps."

To a stranger from the city, the storied slow-and-easy atmosphere of the southern small town is still apparent in Buena Vista. Yet here, too, the pace has quickened and the circle of ordinary travel and activity has widened. During my visit, many of the people I met made trips out of town. Housewives shopped in nearby Americus, and couples went out to *(Continued on page 44)*

Sidewalk spectators rest on fertilizer sacks as they wait for the start of a parade, one of the events in June 1973 marking the hundredth anniversary of David City, a prairie town of 2,400 in eastern Nebraska. For the occasion, the supermarket window displays mementos of an earlier time: a turn-of-the-century typewriter beside a sauerkraut stomper, once used to pack and squeeze shredded cabbage into stone jars; and, next to a pair of hames for a horse collar, a baby picture of Charles Wright. During the centennial celebration, Mr. Wright and his wife, Henrietta, wearing a poke bonnet, take part in one of the style shows. A retired farmer, Mr. Wright considers David City a good place to live: "It's a nice, quiet community with a lot of friendly people." Homemade plaid outfits and a derby for Dad won a first-place fashion award for the Kenneth Chapek family.

LOWELL GEORGIA

41

Sudden shower drenches youthful bystanders at a firemen's contest, as a team chases a beach-ball target with a stream of water. One of the events on David City's centennial calendar, the competition tests speed and skill in uncoiling lengths of hose and connecting them to a hydrant and nozzle. Schoolboys take part in a flag ceremony during the three-day celebration. Escaping the heat of June, Louis Kucera, a retired farmer, and Adolph Patocka, in a felt fedora, join the crowd at Trojan's Sportsman Bar. Eight years before the centennial, in another community endeavor, David City merchants painted storefronts, designed new shop signs, and planted trees to spruce up the decaying downtown. The renovation recaptured local trade from the big shopping centers in Omaha and Lincoln, and boosted business 40 percent in the first two years. Declining sales and deteriorating main streets plague many small towns, and increasingly local leaders turn to refurbishing and redevelopment projects to lure shoppers.

LOWELL GEORGIA

43

dinner in Columbus, almost an hour's drive away. Herman Elliston returned from a fishing trip near Savannah with his brother-in-law; the Jernigans went to a square dance near Macon; the Duncans left for a football game in Florida.

"Folks no longer sit leisurely just relaxing," said Arthur Boyett, a bearded young accountant who teaches at Georgia Southwestern College, 30 miles from his home in Buena Vista. "Families used to get together regularly for big, all-day dinners, shelling peas, making ice cream, singing songs."

Gradine, Arthur's wife, added, "When we came back home after living in Atlanta for five years, we thought it would still be like that." Her wistful tone said more than her words.

But the young couple hastened to emphasize that the town still offers old-fashioned neighborliness. "If our car sits in the driveway for two days straight, neighbors will call and ask if everything is all right," Gradine said. "People still take a genuine interest in one another, and are prompt to help when needed."

I heard many others make similar observations throughout my trip. Friends and neighbors tend the sick, come in to cook and clean during emergencies, share what they have in times of crisis.

"I grew up knowing that I could walk into any house for help if I skinned my knee," said Arthur. He smiled behind his dark red beard. "I also knew that if I did anything wrong, I'd be recognized —and my parents would be sure to hear about it. Whereas in Atlanta, I saw plenty of mischief to complain about, but I didn't know who the parents were, or what their reactions would be even if I told them."

Out on the approaches to Buena Vista, sagging gray shacks, many with tar-paper roofs and broken windows, provide a glimpse of the poverty that has driven many rural Americans from the countryside. Some—though not all—of the shacks are vacant now. For generations they were occupied by sharecroppers, entire families working for a portion of whatever they could produce and barely able to eke out a living. Most of them were black. It was from Tiny Davis that I learned about them, and about the town's black population today.

Curriculum director of Marion County schools, Tiny greeted me at the door in a brightly striped, multicolored caftan. "Yes, my real name is Tiny. You can see I had optimistic parents," she beamed.

When Tiny came to Buena Vista after college in Savannah and graduate school in Atlanta, there were 19 Negro schools in the county, with one teacher to several grades. Then a consolidation took the youngsters from ramshackle buildings where the wind blew up through gaps in the floor, and put them in a modern brick school. In 1970, the black and white schools were integrated.

Acknowledging all that the integrated, consolidated schools have accomplished, Tiny nevertheless feels that in one way the change has left a vacuum in the life of the black community.

"Our schools were once the community social centers," she said. "Now, when the day's classes end, the doors close and stay closed.

"I'll repair anything that comes my way," says Buddy Steward, taking a moment's ease in his workshop at Buena Vista, Georgia. He sharpens saws and sausage grinders, works in wood and metal, and, when he's not busy, will put together a tool or gadget out of old car parts or pieces of machinery. Although hardware and scrap crowd every shelf, cabinet, and drawer in his place, Steward can quickly find anything from small nails to an old hair drier.

NATHAN BENN

That's a minus for integration. Our children and adults miss having a place for social events. They don't have a community hall or country club to fill the void.

"Our community needs recreation facilities, and we need industry for jobs. The sharecroppers around here started to come off the farms in the late '50's. Some found work in plants in nearby towns and went on living around here, riding to work in covered trucks or sharing in car pools. But lots of others left for Atlanta and other big industrial centers."

Today there are few sharecroppers left around Buena Vista. Those who continue to farm either own or rent their land.

Kary Thornton is one of them. He worked hard for his 50-acre place, where he invited me to see how he cooks cane juice into syrup in the old way, using a long, open-pan evaporator over a wood fire. "Only one of my boys farms," he said, "but he just plows a few patches along the road and does other work, too."

For himself, Kary has few complaints, "and most people around me are living better," he said. "We have electricity now, and running water, telephone, and TV."

Yet much of the work for unskilled or semiskilled laborers is seasonal or pays only marginal wages. During the first half of 1973, a total of 748 adults—almost half the labor force in the county—received food stamps or some other form of welfare assistance.

Most of them worked at picking peaches or vegetables or were employed one or two days a week as handymen or maids; but like many agricultural communities in the South, Buena Vista suffers from continuing unemployment and underemployment.

Many of the town's citizens look to industry to bring prosperity. In the last two decades, communities all across the South have wooed industrial firms with promises of low tax and utility rates, cheap land and labor, or low-interest loans. Some, like Buena Vista's neighbor Ellaville, have succeeded in partially shifting their economic base from farming to manufacturing.

Agriculture is still Buena Vista's mainstay. A poultry company, a small egg-processing operation, and a factory making furniture for mobile homes are the only plants in town.

"People are beginning to realize that farming won't carry them to the extent it did in the past," said Cliff Hollis, a tall, blond vice president of Buena Vista Loan and Savings Bank. He was chipping away at the paint on the windows of the new community center, a remodeled Army barracks. All around us the men of the Lions Club swept and mopped, a congenial cleanup squad for the club's newest project.

"Fifteen years ago a lot of people were satisfied with the way things were," Cliff said. "Now I for one have come to see that things have got to change, that we've got to create more jobs."

It seemed clear to me during the next week that at least half the community is convinced of the need for industrial development and growth. Some, however, fear that industry will ruin the town and upset the status quo. And so the townspeople are divided on this as well as other matters ultimately tied to the question of political power.

"I wish the community would do more to attract business," said Wesley Weaver, a hometown success story and one of the two men responsible for Buena Vista's furniture factory. He and his brother-in-law, Larry Chapman, started building cabinets, tables, and chairs for mobile homes in the backyard while they held full-time jobs in Americus and Ellaville. Now they have a plant of their own, with more than 50 employees, in the new industrial tract at the edge of town.

"The people that run things here really didn't do much to encourage me," Wesley said. "If I hadn't been a Marion County boy, I wouldn't have stayed. Some folks have had it one way for a long time, and they don't want it to change."

"Are you too busy to join the Lions Club?" I asked. I had been surprised that he wasn't present at the meeting the night before.

"Well, ma'am," he replied, slowly and carefully, "I just might not agree with their ways. I guess I'm more at home with folks who pay no mind to the proper dress, the proper this and the proper that." He flashed a dry smile that didn't temper the thrust of his jaw or soften his piercing green eyes.

"When I was a boy and coming up in high school, I had 25 cents a day to eat on. Some of those boys in town had their own cars and all the money they wanted. We didn't have much in common. Even after I graduated, the people in town didn't have a whole lot of time for me. They'd just as soon I wasn't in their store. I didn't have any money." Wesley shrugged. "I guess I was more sensitive than some to such as that. But it still sticks in my mind."

At 33 Wesley is a tough, canny businessman, one of the group that one day may challenge those in control of Buena Vista.

For behind the gracious, century-old homes, the square dances, the fish fries and possum hunts, lies a town locked in a feud that storms around two men—one a doctor, the other a socially prominent businessman. Although the continuing quarrel is in part a personality conflict, it has become a bitter struggle for political power. By the time of my visit in 1973 the feud pervaded the community. It dominated conversations. It eddied through the streets in whispered rumors and bitter recriminations. It appeared to be splitting the town apart.

To me the feud seemed strangely intense; people were so profoundly committed. Everyone was drawn in, for in small towns no one is anonymous, no one can retreat from events. Each individual is virtually compelled to take a side.

I strolled through the town square in the early autumn twilight to think about all this. The stores had closed that afternoon, as they always do on Thursday, and even the farmers who customarily meet their friends at the feed warehouse and linger there to talk had left their places along the wall.

I compared Buena Vista's conflict with what I had observed as a resident of a metropolitan suburb. There I live in a relatively small circle of friends, and am involved in only a limited way in the larger community. Factions exist, of course, but none can easily pressure or automatically claim me.

Though I am exempt from such feuds, I pay a price for my privacy. For one thing, I have fewer opportunities to speak out in public debate, to influence civic policy—in short, to participate in local government. Its complex, impersonal machinery intimidates me. But for the residents of a small town, government is no remote abstraction. It is a day-to-day reality, as accessible as the mayor mowing his lawn down the street or the tax assessor trapped in the barber chair.

Until Albert Panzeri retired from a mechanic's job in the city and moved to Plainfield in the Berkshire region of Massachusetts, he had never attended a civic meeting or taken a personal interest in government. "Here, I feel I can accomplish something," he explained. "Problems seem more manageable. I know the town officers; I know where to start."

In Plainfield, Mr. Panzeri may well find himself serving as assistant fire chief or director of civil defense, for traditionally everyone in town is expected to take a turn in office.

Another tradition in Massachusetts government is the town meeting, long acclaimed as the purest form of democracy. To observe one of these yearly sessions, I drove east from Plainfield toward Northfield, which has been holding town meetings for two

NATIONAL GEOGRAPHIC
PHOTOGRAPHER OTIS IMBODEN

Democracy in action: Chester Hooper has the floor at a town meeting in Northfield, Massachusetts. Observing the tercentennial of the original settlement, voters wear clothes with an old-fashioned look.

and a half centuries. En route I stopped at a roadside restaurant to read what an earlier visitor to New England had said about such meetings. Some 140 years ago the Frenchman Alexis de Tocqueville observed in his book *Democracy in America* that "town meetings are to liberty what primary schools are to science; they bring it within the people's reach, they teach men how to use and how to enjoy it."

I had no trouble finding the town hall on the lovely old main street, lined with elms, maples, and spacious lawns. The wide street with its militia parade ground and antique houses conjured visions of patriots marching with muskets, and attics filled with heirlooms. Still, it was a jolt to come upon the gathering of citizens and find them all in old-fashioned garb. To mark the community's tercentennial, the townspeople had turned out for the meeting in granny dresses, bonnets, string ties, and top hats.

At 7:30 p.m. Moderator Corys M. Heselton, a merry-faced man with a fringe of steel-gray hair, pounded his gavel to call to order Northfield's 250th annual town meeting. For the next five hours he firmly upheld the rules of parliamentary procedure and kept debate to the point as some 270 citizens discussed the 50 articles on the agenda, or town warrant.

Most of what came up at the long meeting, though important, was pretty humdrum; but I learned that hasn't always been the case in recent years. Northfield and many other small towns all over the nation have grappled with a whole set of new problems created by real estate developers and the influx of newcomers.

Since the late 1960's an exodus from metropolitan areas by professional people and retired executives in search of five acres and fresh air has threatened to overwhelm many communities. In some cases it already has. Not far from Northfield, across the border in southern Vermont, huge recreation developments carved up the landscape before state laws began to regulate land use.

Towns that used to think of planning and zoning as "big city problems" have had to face up to difficult, often controversial decisions on development, decisions involving public control of private property. Fortunately for Northfield, old-timers and new-comers have pretty well agreed on basic objectives.

"Northfield has its share of newcomers," said Dorothy Pollen, correspondent for the *Greenfield Recorder*, "but they want to keep Northfield the utopia of their retirement dreams. The natives want to guard their heritage — they want the town to stay rural. So almost everyone is determined to preserve the character of the place."

John Carson, a member of the town planning board who moved to Northfield in 1968, wants to protect the corner of old New England he has found.

"No, we can't keep development out," said the tall, athletic president of a technical-instrument manufacturing company, "but we want the growth to proceed in an orderly way."

Until recently, he admitted, the townspeople who wanted the strongest zoning and subdivision laws were those who had come from other places where controls had been too little or too late.

"We saw those places ruined. At first the typical New England farmer, reasonably enough, welcomed the real estate boom as an opportunity to make money. But then the people who moved in on the little back roads needed those roads plowed in winter and fixed in summer, and they needed police and fire protection, and their children needed an education. Providing all those services pushed property taxes way up. So even though most old-timers were dead set against regulations, they now see the need to control growth."

In still another part of New England, the hardy, taciturn lobster-men of Monhegan Island are reconciled to an annual invasion from the mainland — for they know it is temporary, and Monhegan's summer visitors have become a vital part of the island economy. Permitted by law to fish only from January to June, the islanders depend on the summer visitors as a secondary source of income. While boats from the tiny village ten miles off the coast of Maine are lifting the last slatted lobster pots of the season, the summer people start to arrive — day-trip sightseers off the ferry boats, tourists who stay at the white-shuttered hotels overlooking the harbor, and the regulars who return year after year to weathered cottages along the waterfront.

The villagers know that when the fog and wind once more bear the icy breath of winter, life on their rocky perch will return to normal — to the hardships and hazards of lobstering, the gales and blizzards, and the warm friendships and deep bonds of loyalty among the 65 permanent residents.

Douglas Odom, who with his brother Harry has fished for lobster and run the general store for some 30 years, cited an example of the way the islanders work together: "One year we was all ready to start the fishing season, January 1, when one man's engine broke down. So we waited. That's the way we do things; if one can't go on Trap Day, nobody goes. Later, if a man's sick, we take turns haulin' his traps till he's on his feet."

DAVID HISER

Explosion breaks ore loose at the open-pit mine above Gabbs, a one-company town in central Nevada. The company, Basic Refractories, sets off several such blasts a month to supply its plant with magnesite, a mineral used to make heat-resistant firebricks for industrial furnaces. Polishing a pumper truck, volunteer fire fighters keep the 1934 engine shiny and ready for action. "She still runs good," says Clyde Farnsworth, perched on the running board of a newer truck. At the Sandy Bottom Golf Club, Bunny Barredo putts the ball down a path leveled across a "green" of oiled mine tailings.

But in a fishing village on the opposite side of the continent, the boats work the year around, and the townspeople do worry about "outsiders"—in this case, the increasing number of visitors coming to Seldovia, Alaska, to fish, hunt, hike, and camp.

"In summer, tour boats bring in so many people that we've had to start thinking about law-enforcement problems," said Hank Gain as we walked along the dock.

In the frigid October dawn, however, there were no pleasure boats anchored in the wind-whipped waters, only about 20 fishing vessels, a few skiffs and dories, and the clumsy hulk of the harbor master's houseboat.

Perched where the edge of a spruce wilderness meets the sea, Seldovia has no rail or road connection with the rest of the world. The highway ends at Homer, across Kachemak Bay, and the village depends on water transport or the air taxis that fly the 17 miles from Homer to a landing strip just outside of town. In summer, water traffic picks up, and from May to October the state ferry doubles its schedule to two stops a week on the run from Homer to Seward, around the Kenai Peninsula.

On this bleak day, sullen clouds obscured the peaks of the snow-frosted Kenai Mountains, but I was awed nonetheless by the grandeur of the steep evergreen slopes tumbling down to the sea.

It takes really heavy weather to keep Hank Gain in port. His 43-foot *Northern Light* is one of the Seldovia fleet's "high boats," those bringing in the biggest catches. The crew came aboard—Jim McGuire, a former engineering student, and Nick Hoganson, an Aleut whose easygoing charity keeps his wallet empty—and then Hank, hands on the wheel and eyes on the depthfinder, steered the boat beyond the breakwater.

After almost an hour the engine coughed to a halt as we came to a buoy marking one of Hank's crab pots. The trap, hoisted by winch from the ocean floor, yielded a poor catch. It was lowered again and we moved on.

The conversation rambled from boats and fishing to a more general discussion of life in Seldovia. "As far as I'm concerned, a car in Seldovia is about as useful as a horse in Manhattan," Hank shouted. I strained to hear above the drone of the engine, the crackle of the wheelhouse radio, and the whoosh of waves rolling over the prow. "In ten minutes you can walk to any place in town— the beach to dig clams, the pond to skate, the bar to pass the time."

Nevertheless, a good many of the families in the village have cars—a convenience for shoppers at the supermarket, and the means for an outing on the 40 miles of rough logging roads that hug the densely forested shores.

Hank, a wiry, sharp-featured man who had come to Alaska in 1952 with $800 and a carpenter's toolbox, talked about the earthquake of 1964, which dropped Seldovia 3½ feet and tested the townspeople's pioneer resourcefulness and composure.

"As the earth shook, I called to a neighbor standing in his yard with a pipe wrench in his hand. The guy yelled back, 'I'm waiting for this thing to stop so I can connect my oil tank back up.' "

And the time only a month later when high water threatened Hank's house, built on pilings along the slough—the town creek whose churning waters ebb and flow with the tides.

"Friends were over that night to play bridge. We were downstairs, and I went around the room drilling holes in the floor and putting corks in them, and I raised the furnace on blocks. Before long we had more than an inch of standing water, so we played with our boots on. When the tide went out, I pulled the corks and the water drained right out while we went on with our game."

Like other people in remote or sparsely populated places, Seldovians must cope with the unexpected by relying upon themselves and one another. Living where you can't pick up a phone and summon a repairman, a delivery service, or a professional fire department tends not only to perpetuate rugged individualism but also to forge a cohesive sense of community. Volunteer organizations are not unique to rural areas, of course, but I found throughout my trip that in small towns and country districts such groups render innumerable services that could not be provided otherwise: volunteer fire companies and rescue squads, library staffs, park and swimming pool maintenance crews, and countless hardworking committees for special events.

The need for self-reliance affects the role of children, both as individuals and as family members. Thomas Overman, the youthful-looking principal of Seldovia's kindergarten-to-12th-grade school, and his pert wife, Sharon, are impressed with the changes their move from Tucson has brought in their family life-style.

"The boys tackle more things on their own," Tom told me over a supper of ptarmigan—provided by hunters Karl, 12, and Kurt, 11 —and rice, lowbush cranberries, and homemade cream puffs.

"But we also do a lot more things together. Here the outdoors means just that—right outside the house. We put our skates on at home and slide down the hill to the pond; we go cross-country skiing from our front door; we fish on the beach only three-quarters of a mile away. In Tucson I watched a lot of television. Here I read more and visit more. The whole family spends hours on a jigsaw puzzle or game. Our TV set was out of order for six months before we sent it to Homer to be fixed.

"It used to seem important to have a new car every three years. Now I keep a '65 model in Homer and a jeep here. We've been in Seldovia three years, and we still haven't unpacked our good china."

Life is informal and unpretentious in Seldovia. Clothes at a social get-together may be a fisherman's waterproof jumpsuit or the Alaskan tuxedo, a many-pocketed whipcord bush jacket. But it's the frontier atmosphere, not a shortage of money, that keeps things simple, for the fishing fleet provides the town with a high level of income. Actually, money is relatively unimportant in terms of status. Individuals are known and accepted for themselves, for personal qualities rather than the trappings of success. And, as in a family where everyone belongs, there is room for the nonconformist and the maverick.

Take the late Jiminy Crickets, for instance. For years he was one of Seldovia's favorite summertime characters.

"With the first snowfall, he'd go up to Anchorage and break a window to get himself locked up in a warm jail. As a model prisoner, he was put on the food detail and given a rifle to shoot rabbits. They say he cleared Anchorage clean out of cats!"

So goes the story in the Linwood Bar. The popular tavern is one of the best places to hear stories—irreverent pronouncements along the length of the polished bar, nuggets of gossip in the booths along the wall. But I always found people ready to stop and talk at the post office, too, or the grocery store, or just on the street.

On a chill Sunday afternoon, however, the streets were almost empty. The last stragglers were inside the movie house for the weekly matinee. An occasional motorcycle sputtered up and down the sloping roads. Two small boys in parkas and rubber boots were fishing off the dock. Curtis Cameron, a seventh-grader, was trying to coax his pet crow off the roof of his house.

"It's easy to make pets of crows, if you get them as soon as they hatch," he announced. He then convinced me that his crow will ride on his shoulder, peck in his ear, and follow him about, although the temperamental bird refused to perform on order.

Curtis also swims, fishes, hunts, traps mink and otter, sails a skiff, and rides a snowmobile. I was reminded of Tom Overman's comment that Seldovia youngsters do more on their own—and of the observations of another friend, the Reverend William Blackwell, who has worked with both city and small-town children.

"City kids often are so organized in their activities—lessons, trips, meetings—they're so tied up with things to do, that they don't know how to play," Father Blackwell said. "When I go fishing with country boys, they're content just to fish. The city boys immediately want to *catch* a fish; they want it to be like going to a store—getting what you go in for.

"Children should be happy simply wandering in the woods, doing nothing in particular. Kids in small towns are more content; they can enjoy themselves just walking."

The youngsters of Gabbs, Nevada, and their parents have a vast expanse of desert for walking, or hunting, or rock hounding. After the first frost, some families go pine nutting—gathering the tasty seeds of the hardy piñon pines that dot the upper flanks of the Desatoya Mountains to the north. Others go to mountain springs for a week's supply of drinking water. The outing saves the cost of bottled water—Gabbs's well water is heavily mineralized—and provides the opportunity for a picnic, with meat, vegetables, and butter simmering in an iron kettle over a crackling juniper fire.

In summer, swimming and golf also take up some leisure time. But a year-round sport in Gabbs is weekend prospecting—a hobby built on hope, on the possibility of striking a bonanza.

"In a 50-mile radius of Gabbs you can find almost any mineral you can think of—gold, silver, copper, molybdenum, turquoise,"

"I like growing spuds," says Frank Raby, who before retirement owned a general store in the fishing village of Seldovia, Alaska. "It's good exercise, and worthwhile with potatoes costing so much." Mr. Raby, 79, moved to Seldovia from Canada in 1922. Today many newcomers seek the neighborliness and tranquillity of rural life.

said Jack Swanson as we roared down an arrow-straight, two-lane highway to take a look at one of his claims.

Jack belongs to that brotherhood of hard-rock miners who have worked underground. Open-pit miners, considered mere dirt-movers, do not belong.

Like almost everyone else in Gabbs, Jack works for Basic Refractories, whose open-pit mining and milling operation sustains the town. Now in his forties, Jack is a draftsman, but at the age of 13 he was swinging a four-pound single-jack hammer in a gold mine 120 feet underground.

We swerved off the road and followed a vague trail across the desert. Clusters of lemon-yellow flowers added fragments of color to the backdrop of gray-green sagebrush and dun-brown desert floor. Our pickup passed over the crest of one hill, then another.

At the base of a steep incline, we stepped out into the space and solitude of the desert. In the distance mountain shadows cast patterns of darkness on the sunlit landscape. Wind whipped the sand into funnel-shaped dust devils that whirled across the wide, stark valley.

We climbed up the slope to a wooden stake about four feet high. It marked Jack's claim and held the necessary legal form, rolled up and inserted through a small hole.

Here and there I could see small mounds of earth, bruises on the nearly naked land. "Those are waste dumps where men have been working claims," Jack explained. Each year a prospector must do $100 worth of work (in labor and equipment costs) or move 240 cubic feet of earth on each claim to keep title to it. Many of the men in Gabbs hold a dozen claims or more, usually with a partner.

Most of the townspeople live in South Gabbs. North Gabbs has the business district: post office, town hall, gas station, hotel, grocery store. But I found that most of the shopping is done in Fallon at the end of an 80-mile drive, or even 150 miles away in Reno.

Susan Fortune goes to Reno about once a month. "I like to go to stores where I can buy things besides bread and staples," she said, hastening to add: "But I wouldn't live there. Here I know all the children my kids play with, and I like small-town living."

Repeatedly the theme of "a good place to raise a family" was voiced. Mrs. Betty Eaken was making candied apples in the modern kitchen of her mobile home. "We left the San Francisco Bay area because of the drug problem," she told me. "We decided that if we moved to a small town, at least our children would be a little older before they're exposed to drugs."

Mechanic Dale Beller took a $3,000 pay cut to move to Gabbs. "I used to commute about two hours every day, and I just got fed up with it. We're outdoor people, and we enjoy hunting and fishing. And here I can let my youngsters play on the school grounds or anywhere around without worrying. We know all our neighbors. It wasn't like that in Los Angeles."

Sometimes the neighborliness and intimacy breed a preoccupation with gossip. Marjorie Crabill, a trim, efficient secretary, remarked that people moving from metropolitan areas are often taken aback by the extent of the gossip that colors small-town life. "It takes a while to accept the fact that people know your business before you do. But," she added emphatically, "when a person is in trouble there is a closeness in a town like this that you won't find elsewhere."

Still, it seems to Ed Alworth, one of the town's longtime residents, that people keep more to themselves now.

"We used to have some big gatherings—dances and bingo—but not so often any more," he said. "People load up the family in four-wheel-drives or campers and take off. Gabbs is often pretty deserted on weekends. And if there is a good program on TV, people will watch that before they do anything else."

But in Milan, Indiana, not even television can compete with basketball. "Nobody can tell you what Hoosier hysteria over basketball is like," said William (Tiny) Hunt, sports editor of the *Versailles Republican*. "You've got to live it." Tiny, a reserved man who measured his words carefully, nevertheless warmed to the subject and told me about 1954, the "year of glory" when Milan High School won the state basketball championship. "The whole town closed its doors to follow the team whenever it played," he said.

At Arkenberg's Ideal Dining Room—informally known as Rosie's —I chatted with Etta Herbst, a wisp of a woman 85 years old. She,

*Part-time prospector Jack Swanson tests rock on
a claim six miles from his home in Gabbs, Nevada.
After he pounds a sample into powder, he shakes
it in a pan with water to sift rock from heavier
specks of such metals as gold, silver, lead, and
copper. Like many other Nevadans, Swanson, a
draftsman for a mining company, spends spare
time prospecting in the sagebrush desert.
"Although we seldom make a strike, we're out in
the hills, getting fresh air and exercise," he says.*

too, talked about the '54 team. "Reaching the state championship
was about the nicest thing that ever happened to Milan," she said
with obvious satisfaction.

I began to grasp the significance of basketball in Indiana.

A framed poster-size photograph of the heroes looked down
from the wall of the café. Rosie's is a Milan institution, and I had
stopped by to meet the regulars who gather at what the town calls
the Liars' Table. The businessmen come in about 8 a.m. for coffee;
at 8:30 the school bus drivers arrive.

For about a hundred years Milan was a tank town for the railroad. When in the 1940's and '50's steam locomotives gave way to
diesels, the need for water and coal stops came to an end; but by
then Milan had long since become a "Saturday town," a trading
center for the surrounding district. Every Saturday the farmers
came to town to handle their business affairs and buy supplies at
Krick's Hardware, Kirschner's Department Store, the feed store
and dime store and drugstore. They would visit with John (Doc)
Droge, the veterinarian, or stop at the barbershop and talk about
the weather and corn yields and dairy prices, while the women
made their own rounds of shops and front porches and ordered the
grocery staples the family didn't grow itself.

Saturday evening the teen-agers would go to the seven o'clock
picture show. Afterward the crowd shifted to the drugstore or
Rosie's for sodas, and then drifted out onto the streets where
everyone stood around and talked, first in front of one store and
then another.

Today corn still grows just across the road from the new consolidated high school, cows still graze at the town limits, and the
business district looks much the same; but the movie house has
shut down, several buildings on the two main streets are vacant,
and the frame houses with their shady porches and picket fences
are showing their age. The farm population that traditionally sustained Milan has shrunk over the last two or three decades as
machinery replaced hand labor; now its numbers are dropping
again because more and more farmers are selling their land—not

Hefting sacks of peanut hulls, workers unload a freight car at a railroad siding in Milan, Indiana. Farmers will use the hulls as bedding in cattle stalls. Long a railroad town and trading center for farmers, Milan today has lost much of its commercial function and has become increasingly a rural residential community for people commuting elsewhere to work. Studying the Gun Trader's Guide in the family hardware store, Porter M. Krick checks prices to find the trade-in value of a weapon. In apron and garden gloves, Marie Ward, 77, ponders a sodding project in her yard with husband Charles, 90. "It's hard work putting in new grass at our age," she says, "but we're used to doing things ourselves."

so much to big, consolidated farming operations as to subdividers promoting the sale of small residential plots. Like many small towns that are within an hour's drive or so of cities—in this case, Madison and Cincinnati—Milan is becoming less the farming center and more the rural suburb, a bedroom community in the countryside.

Part of Milan's new population occupies a trailer park at the edge of town, where more than 50 mobile homes stand on land that three years ago was open pasture.

Ambling down one of its roadways, I came upon Debbie Hall, a young woman with a pleasant face and shy smile. I introduced myself, and she explained that she had moved from Harrison, Ohio, only three months before.

"We don't know anyone around here except my mother and aunt, who have moved here, too," she said. "I guess I'll go to work in the shoe factory in Osgood. Not that I have to work, but there's nobody around all day. My husband works, and my mother works. On weekends my husband and I go back to Harrison—back and forth each day. We just run all weekend.

"My sisters like it here, though, because the kids at Milan High School aren't smart-alecky. In Harrison just the popular ones got to do things; here the school is small enough so that everyone gets a chance."

Size no doubt accounts for the same democratic tone at Milan's Lakeside Country Club, which isn't large and rich enough to restrict membership.

I was interested in what Milan's changing character has meant to its businessmen. Obviously they can't take anything for granted; for one thing, the new residents have no reason to feel a loyalty to Milan merchants, and many of them continue to be oriented toward the cities. Over a memorable steak supper at the country club, I talked to Bill and Mary Gray Thompson and Bill and Mary Lou Steinmetz.

Bill Steinmetz, a cheerful and animated insurance man, told how he still operates his business "the old Milan way. I tell my customers to pay their premiums when they can. In Milan we look at each other every day; we have to trust each other."

Until a few years ago Bill Thompson managed the furniture factory in town. He acknowledged that "small-town closeness" had both advantages and disadvantages:

"I like the informality. If I went to work in a suit, it meant I was going to Cincinnati that day. I played golf with the men who worked for us; I visited in their homes, and they came to mine. But sometimes this closeness isn't good business. How could I fire a guy who was a good friend?"

"I'll tell you what else isn't good business," boomed Bill Steinmetz. "It's having a captive market too long. Many of us have been spoiled up to now. If someone didn't buy here in Milan, he didn't get service. Besides, there was usually only one guy in town you could deal with. The automobile and the good highways have changed all that."

Small towns like Milan, dependent on commerce, have responded by looking for ways to become more competitive—renovating the business district, trying new merchandising ideas, promoting special events. In 1973 the new Milan Business Association sponsored a sidewalk sale and a bluegrass music festival.

The automobile has been a mixed blessing for the small town. It has enabled customers to travel easily to larger towns and cities, as Bill Steinmetz pointed out, for shopping and recreation—to the disadvantage of some hometown enterprises. But the same mobility has put Milan on the fringes of urban America, making it an alternative place to live for the person willing to commute to his job. Furthermore, some industrial firms have been able and willing to locate on rural sites because they could assume the availability of a mobile labor force.

Recently, of course, a new uncertainty has emerged—the effect on these trends of rising petroleum prices and what may become a long-term shortage of gasoline.

If the fuel shortage does slow or halt the movement of urban Americans toward the countryside, it will frustrate what apparently is a widely held, steadily growing desire. Calvin L. Beale of the Department of Agriculture's Economic Research Service told me of a recent survey showing that some 40 million Americans in metropolitan cities and their suburbs would prefer to live in a rural or small-town environment.

"The records show, too, that the population of towns of less than 2,500 grew by almost 8 percent during the 1960's," he added. "In the South, the average was 14 percent. Despite some regional declines, the facts, nationwide, don't support the general impression that small towns are dying out."

I am not surprised by what the statisticians have found, when I think back to the small-town people I met and the moments we shared. Almost without exception, those I talked with on my assignment were living in a small town by choice, not of necessity. They had come there, or had stayed there, because they preferred to do so. Native or newcomer, each had found his own special satisfaction in small-town life.

Writer Charles McCarry, who has lived in cities in both Europe and America, returned to his native Plainfield for the beauty of the Berkshires, and to give his four sons a chance to grow up among the "hills that have produced an upright people, different from any other."

Bob and Jeanne Jernigan of Buena Vista said, "We like the peace and quiet. And though we enjoy meeting new people, it's nice to walk into a place and know everyone we see."

And with typical Alaskan candor, Billi Kaho told me in her little house by the slough in Seldovia that she likes small towns because she can feel needed and important. For a moment she watched the sea gulls wheeling outside her window; then she said with a smile, "Here in Seldovia I can leave a footprint. We all want that, don't we?"

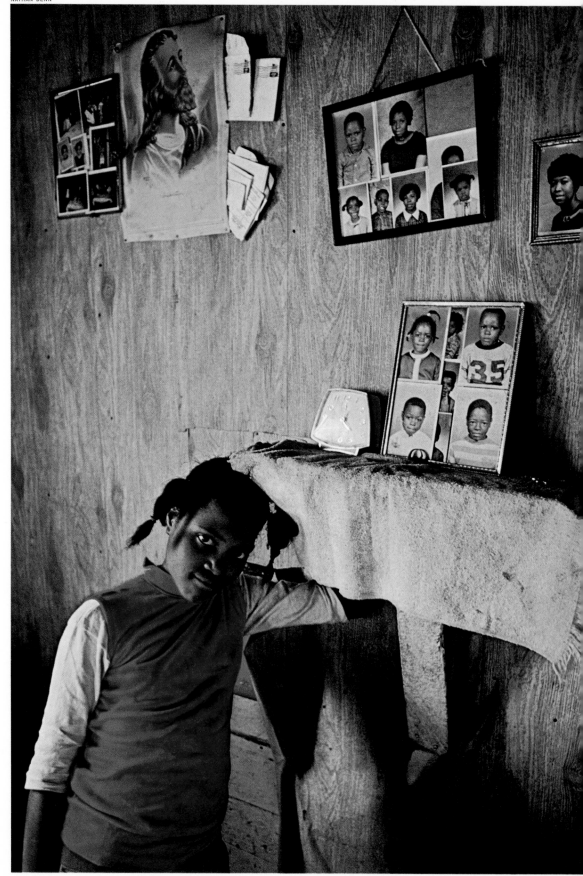

Wistful, 12-year-old Linda Faye Foster shares a two-room house with her mother and ten brothers and sisters in the tiny Delta town of Beulah, Mississippi. Alberta Coleman, who finds work at Beulah as a seasonal farmhand during the summer and fall, feeds the chickens before heading for the cotton fields. Many residents of the town, like Idella Lloyd, resting on her hoe, stretch meager incomes by growing some of their food in small garden plots.

Through a long, sultry afternoon in Buena Vista, Georgia, friends tarry in front
of a feed warehouse, where they gather to talk about prices and the weather and
pass the time of day. Cupping his ear, Jonathan Davis, who has lived almost all

his 101 years in Marion County, enjoys the companionship of Luther Lewis John-son, 85. Grinding sugar cane to make syrup, Gem Nether feeds the mill a stalk at a time as owner Kary Thornton chews mashed cane to be sure no juice remains.

White columns of the Marion County Courthouse and a home's elegant parlor symbolize the grace and luxury of life in the Old South. The courthouse, built in 1850, rises in the center of Buena Vista's town square above a spacious lawn shaded by oak and pecan trees, and serves not only as the center of county government but also as a business and social hub of the community. In her living room, in the house where she was born, Mrs. Esther Short Stevens recalls a vanished way of life. "It would be terrible to have to hustle and bustle all the time," she says. But today she does her own gardening, cooking, and cleaning, and when she could hire no one to paint her garage, she put on her fishing clothes and did the job herself. One of her lingering regrets: "We lost our magnolia trees when the town paved and widened the street."

NATHAN BENN

In an immense field in Oklahoma, a professional wheat cutter and a farmer examine kernels of ripened

Chapter Three

Rural Americans at work: "You're called on to do anything"

grain. Each year harvesters race against the hazards of wind, rain, and hail to bring in the crop.

BY CLAY ANDERSON

The first field lay on the right as we drove slowly down the gravel road. Dad and I were going back to the farm—to the 96 acres he and Mother bought some 40 years ago at the height of the Great Depression. It was there I grew up, the oldest of six children. Neither of us had passed this way for years, but the field still looked much as it did when I was 8 and Dad and I loaded bundles of oats onto a horse-drawn wagon.

In these southern Missouri hills I first saw the hard work that typifies rural life. Now I was taking a new look, here and in other parts of America, at the ways country people make a living—to see what has changed and what seems to continue from one generation to another.

The meadow farther along the road had once grown a profusion of redtop and timothy, grasses we harvested for hay, but now largely supplanted by fescue and other crops of better quality for forage. Beyond, I could see a familiar hickory tree, and beneath it, I knew, was a pond. The location was strategic; our fences intersected, and cattle from four fields watered there. When the pond froze over in winter, my brothers Joe and John and I had to chop holes in the ice so the cows could drink. The reward for our labor was often a game of skateless ice hockey with hickory sticks and a cow-chip puck.

Now it was midsummer, and we were approaching two sloping fields where we had grown alfalfa. For all the familiarity of the land thus far, I suddenly thought we had made a wrong turn. On the hilltop just ahead had stood our rambling old two-story house, and clustered around it the smokehouse, milk shed, chicken house, barn, and silo.

The house was gone. In the middle of the field across the road stood another house, familiar yet misplaced. Once the home of our nearest neighbors, it had been moved intact to make way for a new interstate highway.

On our hilltop a mammoth white oak was missing, but a craggy pine that had been our baseball backstop was still in place; so was a venerable pear tree that had been at the back of the house. Of the buildings, only the milk shed and the barn had survived. Near them was a large metal structure. We took the driveway leading to this new building and encountered its owner, Ronnie Tuschhoff, proprietor of a farm-equipment business.

We asked permission to look around, explaining we had once lived on the farm, and our host obligingly told us what he knew about it. "Some people around here call it 'the Anderson place,'" he said. We had to smile, for in the more than 20 years we Andersons had lived there, it had consistently been known as "the Morton place," for the previous owners. Tuschhoff had bought 30 acres out of the center of our old farm and found that his machinery business did as well in the country as it had in the city. Customer traffic is increased by the nearby Fruitland Livestock Auction, a modern sale barn handling hundreds of head of cattle every Friday. Its operators are Dad's sister, June, and her husband, Harry McDowell, a personable and compulsive trader.

Wandering about, we found a few more vestiges of Dad's efforts to build a dairy farm on a shoestring: the depression of the trench silo where green corn fermented for cattle feed; the concrete foundation that we laboriously poured for the upright redwood silo; the metal hoops that held the redwood staves together like a giant barrel.

I stared at the barn, remembering how I had been propped on a stool to milk a big, gentle red cow the summer before I started to school. Later, it was here that my brothers and I got the overdose of farm work—tending 25 cows twice a day, year around—that helped push us into other careers. For years we milked by hand, and when we finally got a milking machine it was a used one and not too dependable.

Most of the land is in grass now. Some grain sorghum grows in the creek bottom. The bottomland was vital to us; it was about the only part of the farm suitable for row cropping, and I've traveled back and forth across that field with a horse-drawn cultivator more times than my children will ever believe.

Some of the hill fields show the benefits of the terraces Dad built to prevent erosion, at the suggestion of government soil conservation advisers. I remember the shock I felt when these men told us our farm was economically "marginal." I wanted to prove them wrong, and I'm sure Dad did, too; he certainly tried to make the improvements that might enable our family farm to succeed.

In the end, though, the harsh estimate of the government men proved quite accurate.

Ronnie Tuschhoff likes the portion of "the Anderson place" he owns. He hopes to build his home where the old house stood. "That's a pretty spot," he said.

"Yes," I murmured. It still is. But off to the west, the once sylvan view is scarred. Two farms, much larger and more prosperous than ours, used to occupy that ground. The new highway sliced through both, altering or obliterating every trace of what had been there.

It had been a wet, erratic spring, and from the small airplane my friend Larry Price and I could see that many of the fields along the Mississippi and its tributaries were still flooded. But after Larry landed us smoothly at the Muscatine, Iowa, airport and we drove through the flat, black countryside to the Wilbert Stoltenberg farm in Scott County, we found that Bill had somehow foiled the elements and gotten his crop planted.

Rows of corn shoots stretched off to the fences bounding his 160 acres; beyond, the neatly tilled fields of other farms reached to the horizon, broken only intermittently by a tree, windmill, silo, or cluster of farm buildings.

Inside the back door of the big, square farmhouse where he has lived all his 55 years, Bill was shaving his lean, ruddy face with what appeared to be a first-generation safety razor. His farm equipment, however, is obviously not so dated. When I asked how he had managed to get his crop planted under such difficult conditions, he answered, "You go day and night when the weather is

Collecting and boiling maple sap, New England farmers continue an early-springtime chore the first settlers learned from the Indians. In a sugar bush in northern Vermont, Dave Lawrence and Bob Davis pause at each tapped maple tree to empty its attached bucket into a gathering tank on their horse-drawn, sledlike dray. Beneath a fragrant cloud, Royal Osgood tests steaming sap in his Massachusetts sugarhouse. Boiled for hours in long vats, 40 gallons of sap will yield a gallon of thick maple syrup.

good." But he was quick to admit that the ten days it had taken him to get 120 of his 160 acres planted to corn would have stretched to several weeks if he'd been limited to the implements he knew as a boy. Now he has two diesel tractors and the tools and machinery to go with them.

Bill grew up with the concept that one man and his family — with strenuous effort — could take care of 80 acres of the rich Iowa land. But now he was already past the peak of labor on his crop. During the growing season he cultivates the corn just once, "to loosen the soil." Some of Bill's neighbors don't cultivate at all. "Right now I'm waiting for the sprayer," he said, referring to the rented herbicide apparatus he uses to eliminate weeds and grass formerly controlled by four or five cultivations.

What has happened to Bill's operation — the increase in efficiency over the years — is the essential story of modern American agriculture. The pesticides, herbicides, commercial fertilizer, and big equipment he uses are profitable because they greatly increase productivity. Bill's father considered 100 bushels of corn per acre an outstanding yield. Most years Bill averages 150 bushels.

Low corn prices during the 1950's and '60's led the Stoltenbergs to diversify by feeding a portion of their grain to livestock. Bill feeds about a hundred head of cattle each year, and varying numbers of hogs, but this dictates a careful attention to markets and prices. Recently an increase in beef prices gave him a good profit on a hundred head; but once they were sold, he was faced with a much higher price for young cattle if he wanted to repeat the cycle — and thus he had to weigh that course against the improved price he could get for his corn.

Beyond this, there are considerations of steeply rising costs of equipment and supplies, increasing taxes, and the tempting price the farm would fetch on the current market.

"I could sell out tomorrow for $1,000 an acre," Bill said, but it was evident he had little heart for such a move.

In fact, it is difficult to picture the Stoltenbergs in any other setting. Gloria still keeps a few chickens, sells eggs, and plants a garden. Bill clings to vestiges of the farm life he knew as a youth as strongly as he does to his ancient razor. Their adjustment seems eminently satisfactory: On their rich quarter section they have adapted to and benefited from modern farming methods while retaining the small-farm atmosphere they both enjoy.

Aubrey Goodwin of Rosston, Arkansas, would like to grow a 200-pound watermelon. I would like to see one; and I had timed my visit in the hope it would coincide with the start of the melon harvest. Instead, I found the husky farmer and his slim, 13-year-old son, Alan, building scarecrows.

It was midsummer of what so far had been a poor year for melons but a good year for corn. Aubrey farms 193 sandy, rolling acres in southwest Arkansas, planting 12 to 15 acres of watermelons, about an equal acreage of corn, two or three acres of purple hull peas, an acre or two of cantaloupes, and usually an acre of late tomatoes. The rest of his land is pasture for 60 head of beef cattle.

The corn, indeed, looked good—from a distance. But when the pickup laden with its ragtag assortment of scarecrows stopped just across the fence from a field of tall, lush green stalks, I could see the handiwork of the crows. Closer examination showed that the mangled shucks covered mostly bare cobs; the soft kernels had been dug out and devoured.

Aubrey had little idea whether the scarecrows would work. It was simply the only thing he could think of to try to stop, or slow, the loss of his crop. But I soon learned that his melons were equally vulnerable to pests and diseases. A single tour through the Goodwin fields quickly taught me far more than I had ever known about growing watermelons. The job requires a great deal of handwork and an immunity to heartbreak.

About an acre of the Goodwin planting is devoted to trying for heavyweight melons. The effort could be called watermelon roulette. If and when these fruits reach a hundred pounds or so, they bring premium prices from such buyers as resort hotels and sponsors of special events; and here in the vicinity of Hope, Arkansas— self-proclaimed "watermelon capital of the world"—there is a chance at an annual prize of $300 for the biggest melon. Aubrey collected that once with a 156-pounder.

Another year, however, only one of his melons reached 100 pounds, and many other seasons he has had only a few. That was the prospect the summer of my visit. Cobb Gem is the variety that reaches such gargantuan weights, and the virtue of its size is balanced by a susceptibility to disease, pests, and the elements. Most of the rest of the acreage is planted to Charleston Gray— oblong, light green melons that seldom exceed 35 pounds. These bring three to four cents a pound early in the season, two cents a pound or less when the main crop hits the market. A 100-pound Gem, by contrast, commands a price of $15 to $20.

Aubrey worked his way down the middle of the wide, contoured rows, looking carefully from vine to vine. He showed me how moles and pocket gophers can burrow into the roots, damaging or destroying a plant. Some vines in poorly drained spots had been stunted by the more-than-ample rainfall.

Aubrey trains every vine in a row of melons to grow in the same direction, carefully positioning it by hand. This permits him to cultivate a maximum area with his tractor and leaves a fairly open path for vehicles during harvesting.

I was jolted by the number of immature fruits that must be plucked off and discarded. A deformity or severe blemish condemns a melon; so does evidence of disease or damage by pests. It pained me even more to see a ripe melon suffer the same fate. Alan held one up with the same stoical acceptance I had already seen on his father's face. In one end was a jagged hole about the size of a fist. The red meat had nearly all been removed. "Coon," muttered Aubrey.

In a good year, a commercial variety such as Charleston Gray may produce 300 to 400 watermelons per acre. Only in case of drought are these vines closely pruned to remove irregular shapes and other questionable candidates. But with the Cobb Gems, where a mammoth specimen is the goal, a single promising melon per vine is selected and nurtured like a queen bee; all the other fruits the vine sets are pinched off.

"Everything's got to be just right," declared Aubrey, recalling his 156-pound champion. "You've got to plant the vine in the right place, get the right kind of weather, see after it, prune it, keep the small melons picked off—just do everything you know to do."

The master melon was grown on a patch of ground Aubrey rented from a neighbor. "When the weather got real dry," he said, "it just struck me that to make that one grow, I'd sacrifice all my other vines around it, and stir the ground real good. I took the tractor and harrow and went all around that vine six or eight times until the sandy dirt was like a bed of ashes. Then I made sure it got plenty of water."

Aubrey finally picked the melon when he spotted a blemish starting on the underside. Otherwise, he said, it would have gotten even bigger, for the cut vine produced a steady drip of water— evidence that the melon was still growing when harvested.

Aubrey Goodwin bears the frustrations and annoyances of his profession very well. Unflinchingly he tossed aside a hefty melon ruined by a crow peck, and selected a new candidate the size of a baseball. The problems of marketing his produce bother him more. Turndowns from overstocked stores, haggling over picayune points of quality by produce buyers, and sitting at the roadside waiting for individual customers still fill him with notions of expanding his herd of cows and forgetting about truck farming. Young Alan has similar ideas, reinforced by memories of long days spent humped over, picking through the patch. Still, I suspect that the memory of a dripping vine will draw them into the watermelon sweepstakes again and again.

Much of the work done by rural Americans is not farming or ranching, of course. Just as is true in urban areas, more people are engaged in supplying goods and services than in basic production. They keep store, tend the sick, repair machinery, manage banks, hold public office, sell insurance, deliver the mail.

For 37 years my uncle Bill Anderson drove 65 miles a day, much of the time in first or second gear, covering an R.F.D.—rural free delivery—postal route on the rough, rocky back roads around Brumley, Missouri. Six days a week he and thousands like him have made their rounds carrying letters, catalogues, baby chicks, equipment parts, and an endless assortment of other packages. At various times Uncle Bill was also involved in farming, turkey raising, and other enterprises; but his day-in, day-out vocation was providing a link with the world for hundreds of people living along those sometimes snowy, often muddy, usually dusty hill roads. Now, in retirement, he cultivates a huge flower, fruit, and vegetable garden and helps relatives with carpentering and plumbing—and he and Aunt Zella receive their mail from his successor on the same route, Bob Meyers.

The only bank in Ozark County, Missouri, is the Bank of Gainesville. Its president is John Layton Harlin, whose family established the institution in 1894. For many years the banking house was really one man: "Uncle Johnny" Harlin, seventh in a family of eight sons, and grandfather of the present banker.

A civic leader in the best tradition, Uncle Johnny spearheaded efforts to improve schools, build roads, restore a burnt-out church. He served as county clerk, tax collector, treasurer, and state senator. In hard times, when families decided to move away, they would drag a wagonload of possessions to the town square in the county seat and Uncle Johnny would be summoned to serve as auctioneer. Banking hours were extended as necessary; if someone needed money for an emergency at night or on a weekend, he would go knock on Uncle Johnny's door.

He was not a superstitious man, but he became the accessory of those who were. A seventh son, according to the lore of the mountains, could remove warts; and many still say that power rested in Uncle Johnny. He would put aside whatever he was doing and obligingly lay his hands on a believer.

No longer can you have warts removed at the Bank of Gainesville, but Uncle Johnny's son, Hugh, and grandson, John, have continued the emphasis on personal and community service. Both have figured in just about every local organization, plumped for industrial development and school improvements, encouraged tourism and new agricultural methods. Their policy is simply stated: If it's good for Ozark County, then the bank should share in the work and responsibility.

As important as a banker to many a rural community is the storekeeper willing to run long-term charge accounts for those whose income is not weekly or monthly but seasonal. Russell Todd's place of business could be taken for an outdated gasoline station. Actually it's a general store that supplies the Union Flat community of small farmers and timber cutters with groceries and many other day-to-day needs, "from horseshoe nails on up." A large share of the purchases are on credit extended by Russell against the future sale of cattle or delivery of cedar posts or some other payday. In his familiar truck the good-humored, accommodating Todd shuttles between Union Flat and Springfield, Missouri, 60 miles away, to pick up such special-order goods as tractor parts and television sets for his customers.

Our country doctor is still less than 40, and drives a Pontiac. But Dr. William Roston carries on the tradition of unselfish medical care with the same dedication as his horse-and-buggy predecessors. He once ruined a transmission driving across a field to reach a mother in labor. Finding some elderly patients untended, he not only treated them but also cooked their supper. He kept a patient in his family's guest room for several days until the man could be moved to a hospital. Doc charges $4 for office visits, and the only way to find out what you owe is to ask. (Continued on page 86)

NATHAN BENN

Barefoot in soil warmed by the April sun, Arkansas truck farmer Aubrey Goodwin plants seeds in his 15-acre watermelon patch. He also grows corn, cantaloupes, and purple hull peas for local sale. Hard rains and animal pests took a heavy toll of the season's crops after an unusually wet spring delayed planting; but despite such adversities, Goodwin continues to farm: ''I'm crazy enough to plant some more the next year.'' In nearby Hope, Arkansas, market owner Barry Brown inspects a load of corn and watermelons from the Goodwin fields. Inside another store, Goodwin and his son, Alan, check prices on a retail display. When not at high school, Alan helps plant, pick, and deliver the farm's produce.

Hats shielding them from the hot, hazy sun, Mississippi field workers bend over their hoes to weed long rows of cotton. As new technology brings an end to sharecropping, landless workers congregate in small towns. These children in Jones Village, Mississippi, sleep three to a bed, a kerosene lamp and the baby's night-time meal close by. Linda Faye Sayles of Pattison carries water from her uncle's house to relatives next door.

81

Brothers Ray and Melvin Cunningham flank hired hands Eddie Williams and Otis Best on a mechanical transplanter setting out tobacco seedlings. At left, the morning sun backlights creamy white blossoms of a ripening plant. The Cunninghams farm 43 acres of prime North Carolina tobacco land. After breakdown of a harvesting machine, Elizabeth and Jean Cunningham join their husbands in the August heat to pick and load the leaves by hand. The Cunninghams sell about 89,000 pounds of tobacco yearly; by costly investment in new machinery and curing barns, they hope to keep their family farm operating.

SAM ABELL (ABOVE); WILLIAM H. CAMPBELL (OPPOSITE, BELOW);
WILLIAM L. ALLEN, NATIONAL GEOGRAPHIC STAFF (RIGHT)

KURT E. SMITH

Rows of pistachio trees stretch beyond a distant rise behind Fred Andrew, president of California's Superior Farming Company. From his headquarters in Bakersfield, Andrew directs a firm that uses technology and careful management to grow 35 different crops on 37,245 acres of land. The company's equipment includes the electronic console at right, which can regulate irrigation of more than 800 acres at a time. Opposite, a picket holding the black-eagle flag of the United Farm Workers shouts at non-union workers in one of the Superior orchards.

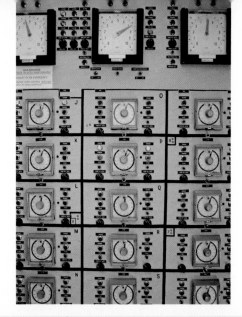

A few years ago when a friend of mine suffered a massive heart attack, Doc Roston covered the three miles from his office in Forsyth, Missouri, in less than three minutes, and saved the man's life. In the midst of great cities I have been confounded by how difficult it is to find a doctor in an emergency. Ours always seems to be on hand when we need him.

The back-to-the-land movement has reached such proportions and variations in recent years that segments of it can justifiably be called cultish, or at least faddist. Jerry Belanger, youthful editor and publisher, has a nonconformist's beard and a zealot's enthusiasm; but the staple of his magazine on country living, and of the 17,500 subscribers it has attracted in less than four years, is old-fashioned practicality.

An iconoclast who worked at two jobs and started a short-lived regional magazine while earning his journalism degree at the University of Wisconsin, Belanger found his greatest satisfaction for several years afterward was to make his one-acre "homestead" in Marshall, Wisconsin, as nearly self-sufficient as possible. In a struggle to keep the regional magazine alive, he acquired a small printing press, and so continued to earn some money from occasional job printing when the publication expired. After working briefly for a telephone company, he signed on as a reporter and photographer for the periodical of a national trade association, then gave it all up when he found he was traveling 100,000 miles a year "and all the hotel rooms and all the airports began to look alike, and all my stories started coming out the same."

Jerry's independent streak was reinforced by the part-time printing business and the amount of food produced on his acre. To feed themselves and their four children, he and his wife, Diane, kept dairy goats, chickens, and rabbits, and fattened and butchered three hogs a year. The animal manure went onto a productive garden that yielded tomatoes, potatoes, and various other vegetables, and apples, pears, plums, and berries.

The further this project went, however, the more information Jerry craved on subjects as diverse as beekeeping, goose feather beds, and the virtues of sunflower seeds. Using his little printing press, he started an information exchange in 1970 — a single-sheet newsletter in which people of like interests could ask and answer questions on what the editor called, for lack of a better term, homesteading.

A single classified advertisement in a national gardening magazine brought more than 200 responses, each containing a dollar for a subscription. Jerry thereafter acquired a nearly defunct domestic rabbit journal, launched a dairy-goat magazine, and with his newsletter expanded to several pages, met himself coming and going. So he merged all his publishing efforts into one: *Countryside and Small Stock Journal.*

Its modest but steady growth reflects the solid, intense interest of its readers and their response to the philosophy of its editor. "We hear from some of the cult types," says Jerry, but he has learned to

White wine ferments in redwood vats at a California winery. James Nichelini, whose grandfather started planting grapevines in 1890, tests for sugar content. At rear, barrels and puncheons store aging wine.

spot their letters: "They just talk. They don't listen. They've got all the answers already." Not so for the bulk of his readers, 95 percent of whom Jerry estimates hold jobs and do their homesteading in free time—and never run out of questions.

Readers ask how to tan leather, how to make cheese from goat's milk, how to use the praying mantis to control other insects. They ask for diagrams for cream separators, and ways to make clay soil tillable. They share information on domesticating wild pigeons, making blood sausage, spinning wool, and processing wild honey.

I was interested in Jerry's achievements as an information broker but even more in his family's actual involvement in homesteading. After nine years on their acre in Marshall, they moved last year to an 80-acre farm outside the neighboring town of Waterloo. Their new home had once been a family dairy farm, and boasts a big, comfortable house and an assortment of barns, sheds, and other serviceable outbuildings. There is shelter for the assorted livestock and poultry, and the printing press occupies part of the barn loft.

As soon as they were settled, Jerry planted a truck garden. My visit fell on a day that culminated the summer's work, and in the late afternoon friends, neighbors, and magazine staff members were gathering. A keg of beer was tapped beside the silo, bratwurst sizzled over charcoal, and garden-fresh vegetables were brought out from Diane's kitchen. Jerry started up a garden tractor that was hitched to a small cart and chugged out to a patch of sweet corn, from which he brought back a load of roasting ears to be placed on the glowing charcoal.

It was a remarkable assortment of people, I thought: retirees and students; young families pioneering a life-style that combines conventional jobs and old-time farm methods; career farmers hoping to pass their way of life to the oncoming generation. All seemed to share Jerry Belanger's contention that the essence of farm life should not be profit but rather a special kind of independence: the harvest of shared labor, the satisfaction of nursing a sick animal back to health, watching a plant or a crop mature, doing for yourself and those you love rather than relying on others.

At dusk, Jerry was summoned to the hilltop near the house where some children had ridden a horse that now refused to return. The publisher-homesteader mounted the balky steed and was rewarded by being pitched off, injuring an ankle so painfully—we later learned it was broken—that he could not walk. Some of the visitors had already left to do their own chores, and thus it was up to those of us who remained to fill in for our host. Some 36 years after I milked my first cow, I was initiated in the art of goat milking.

In the high valley where Shell Creek tumbles out of the Bighorn Mountains of northern Wyoming, I visited the families of two brothers who run a large cattle and sheep ranch by combining modern management concepts with old-fashioned family teamwork. The Diamond Tail Ranch of Howard Flitner and his sons, Dave and Stan, comprises about a thousand acres of irrigated cropland and many thousands more acres of owned and leased grazing land in the adjoining foothills and mountains. But even more impressive to me than the scale of the operation were the participation and responsibilities of the Flitner children.

Driving from Sheridan over the Bighorns, I had seen both cattle and sheep browsing on mountain pasture before U. S. Highway 14 began to descend almost as precipitously as Shell Creek, which it follows down the canyon to the village labeled "Shell—Population 50."

It was easier to find Flitner land than Flitner people that day. The irrigated portion of Diamond Tail looked like an oversize oasis surrounded by mountains and badlands. At closer range the oasis showed its diversity: expanses of corn and other grains, alfalfa, and sugar beets, all laced by irrigation ditches. Great machines, idled by recent rains, stood silent in the fields. There were extensive corrals and stock pens, thinly populated now with the herds on summer pasture. Finally I knocked at the door of a big ranch house and met Mary Flitner, Stan's wife.

Stan, she explained, was up in the mountains with the livestock; Dave was in Chicago at a board meeting of the American Farm Bureau Federation; his wife, Sue, was in Basin, 20 miles away, at the school where she teaches; and her three children and three of Mary's were in class in Greybull. The clan's patriarch, Howard Flitner, had been about to retire "ever since I've known him, but has never had time," his daughter-in-law said; now he had apparently taken the step, and he and his wife, Maureen, were on a long trip to Australia and South Africa.

With only Mary and her youngest child, Danny, at home, I had a chance to ask what it was like to be a Wyoming rancher's wife.

"You're called on to do anything that nobody else is around to do," she replied. That can mean handling a horse, a tractor, a telephoned market quotation, or a perturbed child.

Mary grew up on a ranch near Big Piney, in the cold-winter country of southwest Wyoming. She and Stan met at the University of Wyoming. The Diamond Tail Ranch has been her life ever since college.

Ranch families are accustomed to rising early, but in June the Flitner alarm goes off in the middle of the night. It's roundup time, and the whole family is involved. Breakfast is at 2:30 a.m.; then the horses are loaded to be trucked to the hills. Stan and Mary are accompanied by Carol, 10, Timmy, 9, and usually Sara, 7. Only Danny, 4, escapes a busy day that begins long before daylight and lasts until dark; he stays with Sue, who also fixes the lunches the riders carry with them. Dave's fellow riders are Kathryn, 16, Ellen, 14, and Greg, 12.

The cattle must be gathered and moved a few miles each day toward the high pastures. The drive is not the punishing sort often depicted in movies, for the whole idea is to move cattle gradually enough that they get in plenty of grazing and don't lose weight. Still, there are plenty of obstacles. Electrical storms can be terrifying in the mountains, and any time control of the cattle is lost, a whole day's work goes with it.

Fortunately, all but one of the Flitners love to ride and love the mountains, so the bone-wearying days carry a spirit of adventure. The lone exception is Sue, a native of Massachusetts whose remarkable transition to Wyoming ranch life has not included enthusiasm for horses.

Another chore assigned the Flitner children is much less glamorous. In February and March, when more than a thousand ewes produce their offspring, there are always a few lambs that turn up motherless. The care and feeding of these "bum lambs" for the first few months of their lives is turned over to the youngsters, who undertake the job as a 4-H club project.

At first the lambs need about a quarter cup of milk every three hours or so. "During the day, when the kids are at school, guess who gets to try to make the lambs drink," said Mary.

Soon the youngsters hurried into the house after their long bus ride. Like all children just home from school, these were hungry. Once refueled, Timmy headed for the corral to get his horse and meet his cousin Greg, after being admonished not to repeat an earlier escapade in which the two had "harpooned a skunk." Carol and I set off to feed her prize heifer, won at a stockmen's field day in Cheyenne and named for that city.

As the little girl gave Cheyenne her "smashed oats," there was no mistaking the fondness and pride which had developed. But Mary had told me that such attachments are tempered by reality. "The first time with the bum lambs, they got to know and love each one. Then whenever one would die or be sold, there was a heartbreak. But the second time around, there's a reserve that keeps the children from being hurt so much."

Mary is convinced that being close to the fundamentals of existence—birth, death, growth, physical challenge—makes a ranch a good place to raise a family. The potentially hazardous things the Flitner children do so matter-of-factly are less dangerous because they have grown up doing them.

We were still talking when Stan came home, and Mary busied herself fixing his supper.

Stan Flitner is a lean, hard-muscled rancher with a touch of gray in his dark hair. He has an air of preoccupation from juggling a multitude of details and concerns, but there is an unmistakable warmth when he talks to his family, and a quick perception when he visits with a stranger.

While his brother was in Chicago, he was carrying a double load. Stan normally concentrates on the livestock operations and Dave looks after the farming. Unwelcome rain had held back haying and the chopping of green corn, but there were plenty of other things to be done, paramount of which was the selling of about a thousand head of fat lambs, still in mountain pasture with cold weather approaching.

He read his mail and talked on the phone to livestock buyers before he was ready to eat.

Next morning it was still too wet for harvesting. The interlude was being devoted to work on a large new cattle corral. Stan consulted with Ed Carter about the bull herd; checked with his 18-year-old head mechanic, John Gilmore, about equipment repairs; and inspected several irrigation ditches. But he was back at Mary's kitchen table when his favorite newscaster came on the radio with the day's lamb market information.

In midafternoon Stan announced that he was going to drive up into the mountains to shoe a horse. As our pickup climbed I realized that for him, going to the mountains was a pleasure trip. He was exhilarated, and every sense seemed quickened. He performed the horseshoeing job like a practiced farrier after leading the animal out of a grove of yellowing aspens. When he had finished, he stood silently looking out over the mountain slopes and distant valleys.

"You really like being up here, don't you?" I asked after a while.

"Pretty good, yeah," he replied with a hint of a smile. "This old mountain kind of grows on you."

As we started back, he talked about a philosophy that has guided his family since his grandfather homesteaded here in 1906. "If we take care of the land, the land will take care of us," he said with conviction. That means the careful rotation of pastures as well as scientific cultivation of croplands.

I had mistakenly assumed that irrigation water was the sole factor in making the fields along Shell Creek productive. In explanation, Stan had shown me a barren field the brothers were still trying to ready for planting. Its native vegetation consisted mostly of greasewood, which had to be removed and burned. The

Wyoming ranch hand Joe Burks takes time out to smoke a hand-rolled cigarette. An expert horsebreaker as well as a sheepherder, "Broken-nose Joe," 60, still works as long as 16 hours a day.

land would have to be carefully graded so it could be irrigated; then the soil would be tilled to leach out soluble salts, and organic material would be added.

"The soil conservation people will tell you it really isn't worth the expense. All that kind of soil does is hold the world together," Stan said. Nevertheless, his father and grandfather had shaped a productive ranch out of alkali soil and unpromising terrain.

Evening shadows began to engulf the high mountain valleys as we turned down the canyon highway. Suddenly Mary's voice came over the truck's two-way radio. After a short conversation with her husband, she reported that Dave was home from Chicago, and that Sue was expecting me at their house for supper.

Dave Flitner is no less a rancher than his younger brother; but whereas Stan has always said he would rather be ranching for himself on 40 acres than be tied to the dictates of a big organization, David took a serious look at careers in the military, government service, and big business after graduating from Dartmouth. Once he made the decision to return to the Diamond Tail, however, he has never regretted it.

The ranch holdings and the scale of operation have grown slowly and steadily as the Flitners attempted to develop an "economic unit" large enough to justify investment in costly modern equipment. Aside from what it has taken *(Continued on page 110)*

Growing up on the Diamond Tail

Text by EMORY KRISTOF

Swimming across a sea of sheep, Greg Flitner gropes to find and separate a lamb from the ewes at the Diamond Tail Ranch in Wyoming. Three generations of the family—including Greg and his sisters and cousins—work long hours during spring lambing when the four-week-old newcomers undergo dye-branding and "docking"—clipping of ears and tails—and neutering of males. A lamb in need of an antibiotic gets attention from Greg's dad, Dave Flitner.

Sheep graze a sloping summer pasture on Black Mountain in the Bighorns. Many Wyoming ranchers, including the Flitners, run both cattle and sheep on the same range; the sheep eat the finer grass and thus encourage growth of the coarser plants preferred by the cattle. Stockmen attribute the state's recent decline in sheep production to an increasing coyote population and a shortage of sheepherders willing to live most of the year in a wagon on a remote hillside. The Flitner children learn responsibility toward the livestock early. Timmy lifts one of the motherless lambs he will bottle-feed. Ellen braces while a lamb's tail is docked.

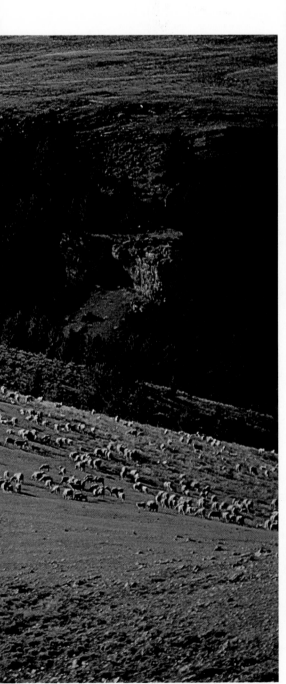

After a long day "pushing cattle," Greg puts away his saddle in the tack room. Ellen and her cousin Mark Fear throw a calf to the ground for branding while its mother glowers. Later, during the drive to summer pasture, Timmy watches Greg test strength with their grandfather. Howard Flitner, a rancher all his life, served in the Wyoming Legislature for 21 years, but has found his greatest satisfaction in the Diamond Tail and his children's and grand-children's devotion to the ranch.

Water duel enlivens the day's work as Kathryn Flitner and another contestant get their steers ready for the 4-H competition at the Big Horn County Fair. The friend's black Angus gets caught in the crossfire. A year of preparation culminates each August in the stockjudging at the fair in Basin, the county seat. Eyes tightly closed, Kathryn's Hereford (opposite) endures a face washing before entering the show ring to win first place in its class. Still too young to raise and handle a steer, Kathryn's cousin Sara takes comfort in petting Sheila, her Shetland pony.

Stretched between stirrup and horns, a bulldogger at the Basin fair's rodeo tightens his grip and prepares to dig in his heels, bring the steer to a stop, and twist it onto its flank. A rugged test of timing, technique, and strength, bull-dogging also requires teamwork by cowboys and well-trained horses; the hazer and the bulldogger's horse keep the steer running straight until the dogger leaves his saddle. Partnership of humans and horses remains a basic fact of ranch life despite increasing mechanization. Opposite, Kathryn and Greg Flitner talk with Joe Burks about the registered quarter horses Kathryn has bought with some of her 4-H prize money. Burks acted as her adviser on breaking and training them.

Not everyone can win, Greg realizes after listening to the judges' announcement. His Uncle Stan's hand on his shoulder consoles him as he tries to hide his disappointment. After the first round of judging, Kathryn and Greg wait in a barn with Mike Michelena for the next call. Ellen's steer (at bottom), like Kathryn's, won in its class. Greg's came in second, but he received an award for showmanship.

Heart of the Diamond Tail lies in the narrow valley of Shell Creek. Corn and alfalfa grown

in the irrigated fields supply winter fodder for herds that summer in the Bighorn Mountains.

Each school day Sue Flitner leaves the ranch to teach first grade at Basin
Elementary School. Her husband, Dave (opposite, above), presides at a meeting
of the Greybull school board on a Sunday morning after church. Like their father,
Howard, the Flitner brothers believe ranch people should represent agricultural
interests positively through public service and political action. Dave serves as
president of the Wyoming Farm Bureau, Stan as vice president of the Wyoming
Hereford Association. In charge of the Diamond Tail's bookkeeping, Mary Flitner
enlists the help of her children—Carol, Timmy, Danny, and Sara—and accepts
an occasional suggestion from her husband, Stan. With each check she signs, she
encloses this message: "Payment of this bill was made possible by the sale of beef."

Harvesting and chopping green corn for fodder, some of the expensive machines essential to modern agriculture move across a Flitner field. Pitting education, initiative, hard work, and long-term planning against the challenges of nature, rising prices, and shortages—from experienced hired help to gasoline and fertilizer—the Flitners keep their dream alive: a successful ranching operation to pass to their offspring. "We plan not only for one generation, but for the next as well," says Dave. "We only hope we can hold it together for the kids!" Greg grins from the back of a feed truck. His roots go deep, and learning his future profession started early; someday he will determine the time to plant corn, the time to sell sheep, what to do about predators, how to finance an improvement. But for now, Greg thrives on the daily adventure of growing up on the Diamond Tail.

to live, everything three generations of the family have earned has gone back into the ranch. Meanwhile, Dave has taken on numerous public responsibilities, ranging from the school board to the board of the American Farm Bureau Federation. The once staid Farm Bureau is developing policies on medical care, international relations, energy utilization, land use, the metric system, fair trade, and the environment. "We've got to have the type of leadership in agriculture that will set a pace for society—not just react to issues," Dave declared.

During the evening, Stan called to tell his brother that he had sold the lambs, and to ask me if I wanted to go with him to the sheep camp the next day.

By morning the wet weather seemed to have ended, and while my host of the evening before turned to organizing the harvesting of hay and corn, Stan, Danny, and I headed into the high country, this time going far off the highway on steep rocky trails, past a sawmill, finally reaching a covered wagon—roofed with aluminum instead of canvas—that is home for sheepherder Joe Martinez.

Stan's purpose was to move the camp and plan for the loading of the lambs on trucks the following Tuesday. Martinez, a slim and supple 65-year-old Mexican-American, has been herding sheep for four decades, with time out for service as an 82nd Airborne Division paratrooper in Italy. He stowed his gear away neatly, buried his garbage, and rode his horse to the new campsite while Stan's truck pulled his wagon. His predecessor with the Flitner sheep, Joe Burks—now working for a neighboring rancher—stopped by to visit. The weathered cowboy-sheepherder has a standard opening question with which to test strangers, Sue Flitner had told me: "How much will you take for your horse?" Those whose horses are not for sale get highest marks with Burks.

When his wagon was repositioned, Joe Martinez fired up the little wood stove and warmed a pot of pinto beans and ham which we devoured with tasty white flour tortillas and pepper sauce.

From the mountaintop we could see the Flitner ranch head-quarters some 20 miles in the distance. We would be back there in less than two hours, but Joe would be many weeks moving his camp a few miles at a time out of the high country.

"I'll be back up Monday night, and we'll ship Tuesday," Stan said. Joe waved and turned back to his sheep.

The secretary who answered my long-distance call was courteous but firm: Mr. Andrew was out of town and not expected for a couple of days; he would be very busy when he returned; perhaps I would like an appointment for some time in the future. I had telephoned the Bakersfield offices of Superior Farming Company during a visit to the West Coast because I wanted to see just what was going on in large-scale corporate agriculture—the much-publicized entry of big business into farming and ranching.

Many of the ventures, I knew, had not fared well, and some of the investing companies had sold out. But Superior seemed to be growing steadily, and I wanted to know more. By being persistent, I managed to arrive at a very satisfactory compromise with the secretary, Kay Kaiser: She would introduce me to the company's operation, and then I could talk to Fred Andrew, the president, on his return.

Over the next two days Kay provided me with printed data, answered scores of questions, showed me color slides, and drove me through several hundred square miles of southern San Joaquin Valley for a sampling of the company's lands and people.

Superior Farming Company, subsidiary of The Superior Oil Company, was started in 1968 and had grown to more than 37,000 acres by the time of my visit in the autumn of 1973. Most of its operations are in California, primarily between Bakersfield and Delano with additional lands in the Fresno and Indio areas. It also has a "controlled-environment" project near Tucson, Arizona.

About a third of Superior's acreage is in alfalfa, cotton, potatoes, and other vegetable and field crops, and the rest in vineyards and orchards — nuts, citrus, and stone fruits.

For a large company seeking to diversify, farming in the rich San Joaquin Valley with its year-round growing season would seem to offer almost unlimited potential. Superior Farming has crops going to market in every month of the 12, even though many of the company's plantings have not yet come into production. For example, some 1,400 acres of pistachio trees are still too young to bear; fig production is less than a tenth of what it is expected to be at maturity; almond output is only a third of what is anticipated.

Along with developing new plantings, the company has acquired many established orchards and vineyards. These, as much as the new fields and groves, are subject to company efforts to get maximum production and quality through every technique deemed feasible by a staff of experts: agricultural and irrigation engineers, entomologists, agronomists, horticulturists, and chemists, backed by a sophisticated system of computers.

The nerve center of the operation is a modern office building in Bakersfield, 12 miles from the company's nearest field. From there we set out in a company car with Kay at the wheel. I soon learned to recognize Superior property by the orange and beige markings on corner posts, irrigation pipes, buildings, and vehicles.

"Unit 1 to Unit 100," Kay said into a radio microphone. "Hi, Art, what's your location?"

Art Soliz, general superintendent of farming operations in the Bakersfield area, met us at an 800-acre almond ranch that was in the midst of its irrigation cycle. The automatic system is monitored from a large electronic panel of lights and switches in the ranch's control house.

Out among the almond trees we found assistant foreman Leroy Simmons. A tall black man who left a Los Angeles aircraft plant seven years ago to try working on a farm, Leroy has "been right with almonds all that time" on this same property — with its former owners and now with Superior.

Art Soliz showed us one of the most significant new techniques:

drip irrigation. An American of Mexican descent, Art went to work as an irrigator in vegetable fields when he was 15. Later he worked for Fred Andrew on a corporate farm in Arizona. As the Bakersfield-area superintendent he has responsibility for 34,000 acres and 1,200 employees. He explained that Superior first learned of drip irrigation four years ago from a farm adviser who had visited Israel. A system of underground pipes feeds emitters which drip water, at a rate of a gallon or two per hour, to each individual tree. There is no run-off and no waste.

Although Art Soliz has risen from irrigator to general superintendent, one thing hasn't changed: He still puts in a long day. To carry out the necessary planning and supervising, he works 12 or 13 hours and drives more than 200 miles. "On a farm, when you finish one thing, you go to the next right away," he explained.

So Unit 100 roared off, and Kay and I drove to the company's mammoth new huller to see the last of the almond crop going through. In charge of the machine was Ronnie Dickinson, a former welder who had joined the company only 60 days before, just in time to be in on the huller's final installation.

Like other modern, integrated farming operations, Superior not only employs technology but also uses the modern corporate equivalent of old-fashioned rural ingenuity. The huge pile of almond hulls Dickinson and his crew had churned out would be utilized for cattle feed. In many of the orchards, cover crops are grown between rows to hold the soil, shade young plants, preserve moisture, and add to income. In areas of strong prevailing winds, young pistachios and other trees are planted at an angle—leaning into the wind—so that when their roots are strong their trunks will be straight. Hormone plant-growth regulators are used to produce large fruits to meet demand at special seasons. And the company operates its own nursery, starting young trees and vines by the hundreds of thousands.

Back at headquarters, Kay Kaiser glanced into her boss's office and gasped. Dr. Henry B. Chavez, plant pathologist and vice president for technical services, had laid out a grapevine on the thick carpet. Accidentally dislodged when a pipeline broke, it had been brought in as an example of the root development achieved through drip irrigation. Planted only eight months before, the vine now had a mass of roots that extended more than five feet— roughly triple the size of a conventionally irrigated plant, Dr. Chavez said.

Kay thought it was hideous. Fred Andrew, when he got back to his office the next afternoon, thought it was beautiful. He had been in Tucson installing a young, new manager at Superior's greenhouse-like tomato factory.

"I'd love to be starting out at 27 in that project down there," he exclaimed, and went on to explain the Tucson operation—a commercial application of a controlled-environment plant-growing technique pioneered by the University of Arizona.

Started by another company as a joint food-production and water-desalinization project, the facility had recently been acquired as Superior's first agricultural property outside California. Tomatoes are grown in a humid 11-acre enclosure sealed in plastic to permit recycling of the water supply. The university's nearby Environmental Research Laboratory has assisted with similar projects in Sonora, Mexico, and on barren Sadiyat Island in the Persian Gulf.

Andrew, 47, is the son of a Long Island lawyer. His plan to attend West Point was altered by a severe accident while in Army service in Germany, and he decided instead to study agriculture at the University of Arizona. His first job was for $270 a month on an uncle's farm, but before long he and a friend persuaded a banker to lend them the down payment for 480 acres. Eventually they sold at a profit, Fred was hired by a large Arizona farm operation, and he's been farming for corporations ever since.

Much of the technology his company is developing will become outdated in due course, Andrew said. "We've got to keep developing new methods and bringing along new young people, or we're going to be in trouble."

Fred Andrew is interested in people who can get things done, and that is why men like Art Soliz, Leroy Simmons, and Ronnie Dickinson have made such a rapid rise.

Superior Farming is not the largest of the corporate farmers in California, but its growth has been meteoric. And it can continue to grow, said its president, as long as it can find capable, enthusiastic, willing people to work on its lands. His own eight children have learned—from a father who still habitually gets up at 5:20 a.m. —what it is like to work on a farm. "I would like for some of them to go into this sort of career," Andrew said. "There are just not enough people in it."

The annual "wine issue" of the weekly *St. Helena Star* was on sale when I visited the Napa Valley north of San Francisco. Vineyard acreage had expanded more than 50 percent in five years to a total of 18,500 acres, the newspaper said, and it predicted that by 1975 all land suitable for growing grapes in the 5-by-20-mile valley will have been planted.

Several famous wineries are located near St. Helena, but I headed instead for the secluded property of Jim and Rosemarie Nichelini, who make about 10,000 gallons of wine a year in the little stone winery Jim's grandfather established in 1890. The Nichelini Winery is in Napa County, but tucked away in Sage Canyon several miles from the much-publicized principal wine district. So remote was my destination that I turned back twice, certain I had gone astray. On the third try, after a steep climb through hills partially shaded by scattered oaks, I came abruptly to a large old house, some sheds, and a sign that told me I had arrived.

Anton Nichelini, an Italian Swiss immigrant, came to this area to mine and homestead in 1884. His mail-order bride, Caterina, selected the site for the house and winery because it resembled her home in southern Switzerland. The lower story of the building is the winery, constructed in 1890 of heavy, hand-cut sandstone blocks, some of them two feet thick and all laid without mortar.

Part of the fermenting shed is of recent construction, and in front of it at the roadside is a new crusher to receive fresh-picked grapes; but almost everything else in sight has the look of age. The original cabin of Anton and Caterina is still on the property, and the outdoor oven where she baked bread—a loaf went with each miner's daily ration of a half-gallon of wine—is still intact.

I saw no clue in the rugged canyon to indicate where the grapes for that early-day wine came from. But huffing my way up the steep, overgrown hillside above the winery, I finally found the stumps of the vineyard Anton Nichelini once cultivated with a team of horses.

A mile or so past the winery, the canyon opens into Chiles Valley, a miniature of the Napa at somewhat higher elevation and the site of Jim Nichelini's home and 80-acre vineyard.

Anton Nichelini never quite understood Prohibition. As a consequence he was apprehended making wine, and after repeal was not permitted to take out the bonds necessary to start up the winery. So his son, William, a civil engineer, did so and planted the vineyard in Chiles Valley. By the time of William's death in 1959, his son, Jim, was caught up in the family tradition.

Aside from the harvesting of grapes, for which the same small group of workers appears each year, this is a family operation. Jim has several tractors for cultivation and a sprinkling system for frost protection, but most of the work—pruning, budding, grafting, suckering, and finally the picking—is done by hand.

In the winery, too, the product is still made in the time-honored fashion, by natural process. There is the new crusher; and a custom-made pump dubbed "Little Wino" moves the wine from the fermenting vats to oak or redwood barrels.

Anton Nichelini made just two kinds of wine, red and white, and sold it mostly in barrels and half-barrels. Jim has responded to the growing demand for varietals—wines made predominantly from, and named for, a particular variety of grape—and he sells only in one-fifth-gallon bottles, mostly right at the winery. The Nichelini white varietals are Chenin Blanc and Sauvignon Vert; the reds are Zinfandel, Gamay, and Petite Sirah. Jim's generic wines are Chablis, Vin Rosé, and Burgundy.

I quickly discovered that Jim Nichelini and his family are independent, hardworking, gregarious, fun-loving people. On weekends and holidays they open the winery to visitors, and what they call "the only outdoor tasting bar in California" is set up under the huge beam of a no-longer-used Roman wine press at the winery entrance. Many of the people who appear are old friends on outings from the San Francisco and Oakland areas, but newcomers too are quickly caught up in the conviviality. There are picnic tables and a barbecue grill under the spreading walnut trees.

The weekend festivity gives way to a never-ending variety of tasks in the vineyard—a joint venture with a cousin—and the winery. But hard as they work, Jim and Rosemarie love every day of it, and if they have a major concern it is wondering whether their son, Jim, Jr., will choose the occupation they enjoy so much. At the time of my visit he was serving in the Army, and with an independence typical of his clan he had not announced his plans for the future.

"I think he'll come around," said his mother.

At Sunnycrest Acres near Chetek, Wisconsin, Allan and Pat Johnson and their two sons moved about the big barn in the practiced teamwork of feeding and milking 60 Holstein cows. It was November, and the streams and lakes of north-central Wisconsin were already covered with ice. The conditions and the twice-daily tasks were remarkably reminiscent of my own boyhood a quarter of a century ago.

"It's not hard or anything," said 15-year-old Dan Johnson. "I just get sick of doing it." He had three electric milking units, and his father was running three others. The routine was to clean each cow's udder, hook onto the pipeline system, attach to the teats— and in less than five minutes repeat the process. With six units, two milkers can handle the entire herd in about an hour.

"It doesn't take a lot of time—that's the best thing about it," said Dan. What bothers him more is the frequency—twice a day—and the hours: a daily struggle to be in the barn at 6 a.m., with a day of school to follow and the all-too-repetitive chore in the evening for a young man who wants to make the high school wrestling team. It can be done though, for Mark, 17, played football and kept up his chores; and the boys are spared riding the school bus, for by driving to school they can leave later.

The evening round had begun with Allan flipping a switch that dropped yeasty-smelling chopped corn out of a silo into a cart. Allan and Pat dispensed feed in front of each stanchion, while Mark and Dan spread oat straw for bedding for each cow. The cows started coming in—some eagerly, others testily—and were fastened in place for the night as the stanchions were snapped shut. While Allan and Dan ran the milkers, Pat fed the calves, kept at one end of the barn, and Mark took care of other livestock.

By using only registered bulls and by systematically eliminating poor producers, the Johnsons have built a herd that averages 14,000 pounds of milk per head per year, with some outstanding cows producing as much as 20,000 pounds.

For the first 24 hours new calves nurse from their mothers, and then are taught to drink from a bucket. When one calf was reluctant, Pat put her fingers in its mouth and forced its head into the bucket so that, as it sucked her fingers, it would learn to drink. It was just the way we used to do it in Missouri.

Pat was reared on a small farm only a few miles away, began doing chores as a girl, and has never really stopped. Even when her five children were small, her younger sisters stayed with the family and she could help out at the barn. As the two older boys have grown and become available to help their father, her role has decreased somewhat, but she still finds plenty to do. The boys had to be in school in October when Allan was harvesting 40 acres of corn, so Pat operated the equipment that chopped the ears and raised them into the silo.

Haying is the busiest time of the year. The first cutting of the 120 acres of alfalfa goes into a silo. Mark usually does the cutting, Pat runs the chopper, and Allan unloads. The second cutting is baled, and Pat and Dan operate the baler.

In addition to corn and alfalfa, the farm has about 35 acres of oats, source of grain and bedding straw. The rest of the 360 acres is in pasture.

The family produces a good share of its own food—milk, steers for butchering, and a large patch of sweet corn. Allan's father, who lives nearby, is an avid gardener and gladly exchanges fruits and vegetables for beef and sweet corn.

Pat's passion is horses, and her contagious interest has passed to the entire family. Each member has a favorite mount among the dozen Appaloosa mares, geldings, and colts that pasture with the dry cows and heifers.

When we had been in the milking barn a little more than an hour, the activity quieted. The last of the milk had coursed through the pipeline into the 520-gallon bulk cooling tank. The cows were losing interest in their feed, sipping from the automatic waterers, and starting to lie down on the straw and chew their cuds. Full stomachs had calmed the calves. Allan deftly cleaned the milking equipment and soon had it ready for the next morning.

Dan and Mark headed for their rooms to study, but Allan joined Pat at the stable of a favorite colt. He spent most of the next hour— almost as much time as it had taken to milk—trimming the colt's hooves. Then he took a last look around the barn, pushed some scattered feed back in reach of the cows, turned out the lights, and followed his wife to the house—that haven of warmth with its lingering aroma of coffee and good food.

The Johnson dairy farm is larger and better financed than was ours back in Missouri, but I was nevertheless struck by the similarities. We bundled up in as many layers of old clothes as the weather demanded, divided up the work, and stayed at it as a team until we, too, could retreat to the warmth and cheer of the house. It took us longer, of course. Modern equipment makes a great difference.

It changes other aspects, too. I found the health inspector's report tacked to the wall of the Johnson's milk house. There were only a few minor items checked for correction. We had lived in dread of the unannounced visits of the milk inspector. He eventually had forbidden us to store hay above the milking area, whitewash the interior of the barn (because of possible flaking), milk in clothes that were not clean, keep nursing calves adjoining the milking area, or bed our cows down in the milk barn in severe weather. More than a quarter of a century later, the Johnsons do all of these things, and they are practical and accepted. The difference is that the pipeline milking system conveys the milk antiseptically clean from cow to stainless steel tank, and then every day or two on into a tank truck that takes it to a creamery.

In a Wisconsin cornfield, county agent Harry Vruwink checks the crop for insect damage. Vruwink has worked in Barron County for 27 years, helping farmers solve livestock, field-crop, and horticultural problems. Through nearly 7,000 such agents the Cooperative Extension Service, jointly administered by the U. S. Department of Agriculture and state land-grant universities, offers farmers assistance based on continuing research programs.

And no longer is it necessary to dig frozen silage out of a drafty silo by hand, to pick corn by hand and store it where rats can tax the harvest, or to clean a multitude of rubber and steel milking-machine parts.

Those of us who left our farms behind have missed out on the satisfactions of such improvements. But the people who are left there still work hard, and they have continued to face a perennial problem: uncertain prices for what they produce on one hand, spiraling costs of supplies, equipment, and land on the other.

An Arkansas friend once told me that farming takes a combination of faith and fatalism, and I saw it in Aubrey Goodwin's chucking watermelons aside, in Allan Johnson's report of the mysterious death of one of his best cows, and in Jim Nichelini's loss of three consecutive years of his wine-grape crop. Less than five percent of the nation's population lives on farms, and the preponderance of those people are there because they very much want to be. That is certainly true of Jerry Belanger and his homesteaders, who persist in blatantly ignoring profit; but it is equally true of Dave and Stan Flitner, who have strived so mightily to put together an "economic unit."

An economic unit that can survive in the changing patterns of modern agriculture is a common goal, although the criteria of Bill Stoltenberg and his neighbors are certainly far different from those of Fred Andrew and the Superior Farming Company. What they all require, however, are tenacity, willingness, and dedication — qualities that somehow seem not to diminish among the men and women of rural America.

Cutting a swath between tasseled corn and verdant alfalfa, Wisconsin dairy farmer Allan Johnson harvests winter feed for his livestock. Chopped green corn and the first alfalfa crop become silage; a second cutting of alfalfa will go into the barn loft as hay. Later, 35 acres of oats will provide grain. In the foreground, Johnson's daughter Julie leads a horse toward the barn. The family's five children all help on the farm. With practiced hands, Mark and Julie shuck roasting ears. Dan and his father repair a wooden fence near the house, more decorative than the barbed and electric wires that fence most of the property.

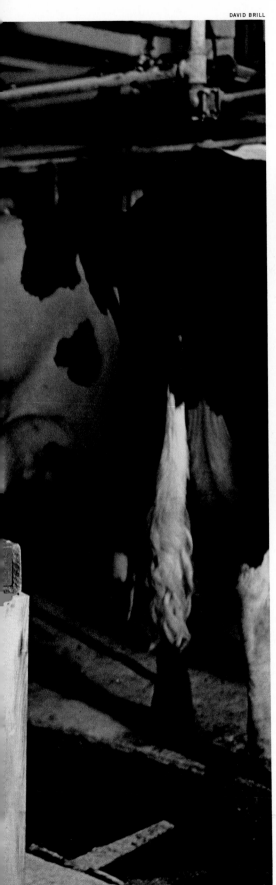

Standing behind part of their herd of 60 Holsteins, Allan and Patricia Johnson complete a monthly check of each cow's production. Jars in the tray contain milk samples for butterfat testing. Johnson holds part of a pipeline milking machine that carries milk directly from the cow to a bulk cooling tank. Elbows on the counter at a feed mill in Chetek, Wisconsin, the dairyman reviews his order with Harold Isaacson and Earl Swanson. They will grind his crop of oats and mix it with corn and specified nutrients.

A quiet moment for a special friend: Patricia Johnson strokes the nose of April, a registered Appaloosa filly. Along with household and farm chores, Mrs. Johnson raises two to four colts a year, maintaining a herd of about a dozen to show and sell. After taking the horses to a professional trainer for breaking, she and her daughters, Vicki and Julie, train them for riding. Last year their entries won 12 horse-show awards.

Sack racers lurch along a dusty course during the annual Thunder Mountain Days celebration in

Chapter Four

Leisure time:
"The sharing of happiness"

Cascade, Idaho. The old-fashioned Fourth of July includes a parade, barbecue, and horse racing.

By Ronald M. Fisher

Appropriately—for this was Idaho—most of the potato sacks had that state's name emblazoned across the front. The competitors, up to their waists in burlap, came huffing through a rising cloud of dust toward the finish line, squirming and lurching like wriggling caterpillars somehow raised on end. Casualties sprawled forward onto their elbows, tripping those behind. The winner was presented a dollar.

It was the sack race for boys 8 to 10—just one of a series of events on this Fourth of July. There had been three-legged races, bicycle races, footraces. During the toddlers' tricycle race one rider, too young to comprehend, never left the starting line; he sat sucking his thumb and staring in astonishment at his father, who kept shouting at him, "Pedal! Pedal!"

Recreation and relaxation in rural America: How do country people spend their leisure time? Even as I set off to ask the questions, I knew some of the answers—for rural Americans entertain themselves to a considerable degree with the same hobbies, the same television programs, the same books and movies that their city and suburban cousins do. They, too, follow professional football and go to conventions and maybe save up for a charter flight to Europe or Hawaii.

Yet there are real differences, obviously, in their circumstances and environments. The countryman lacks easy access to metropolitan museums and theaters and concert halls; but he is that much closer to wilderness, to trout streams and campgrounds and mountain trails. And just as he is slower to change in other ways, so he is less likely to embrace the new and faddish in his leisure-time pursuits. He tends to cling to traditional activities, finding satisfaction and security in the familiar.

For instance: Every July the little town of Cascade, Idaho, turns itself inside out celebrating Thunder Mountain Days, a name intended to evoke the period around the turn of the century when men mined gold from the nearby mountains.

It's a wonder the event ever became a tradition; for though the first celebration in 1938 started off well, it turned into a fiasco. Big tents held gambling tables, a saloon, game booths, shooting galleries, and snack bars. For two days the money rolled in as the townspeople and visitors gambled and the liquor flowed. Then, at 11 p.m. on July 3, a transformer failed and all the lights went out. During the night four inches of snow fell, the tents collapsed, and someone stole the rest of the whiskey.

On July 4, of course, nobody came to celebrate, and when it was all over the Cascade Commercial Club found itself $1,600 in debt.

But the next year the community tried again with better luck, and a July 4 observance has been an annual event ever since.

Located in aptly named Valley County, Cascade is 75 miles north of Boise on a road that winds through hot, dry foothills, then rises alongside the Payette River and abruptly enters the pines and firs of Boise National Forest. In that distance you see only two towns of any size: Horseshoe Bend, after about 25 miles, and finally Cascade.

There seemed to be little danger of snow as I walked through town on my way to the Masonic Hall, where the ladies of the Eastern Star were serving a Buckaroo Breakfast. The smell of sausage cooking greeted me at the door.

In the kitchen, Ann Scrivner had been frying eggs since 6:30. "We've had to go to the store three times," she told me, drying her hands on her apron and brushing back a strand of hair. "So far we've fried 46 dozen eggs and used 40 pounds of pancake flour." At long tables, the citizens were eating everything in sight. I joined Lee Judy, the amiable young banker who was the celebration's general chairman. He looked a little wan, I thought. He said he had had only three hours of sleep.

"I was helping get the barbecue started," he explained. "It has to cook about nine hours, so we had to put it in the ground by three this morning for it to be ready at noon." He described the big barbecue pit the committee had dug. "We need one large enough to accommodate 800 pounds of beef. On the bottom is a bed of coals about two feet thick; we add a foot or so of sand, then the beef wrapped in foil. Then we cover the whole thing with more sand and a metal lid—and keep our fingers crossed."

By 11 a.m. the hot sun was making life uncomfortable for the crowds lining both sides of Main Street. Promptly on the hour, the vanguard of the parade rounded a bend and headed down the hill into town. Children were first, wearing costumes reflecting the days of the gold mines. One, nearly immobilized by his contraption of chicken wire and gold-painted foil, was obviously a nugget. Youngsters not in the parade darted like attacking Indians to gather up the candy and wooden nickels being tossed from the floats. There were a good many horses in the parade, and two little boys equipped with wagon and shovel followed along behind. I wondered how they were elected to this office.

When the flag bearer came marching by, the loudspeaker blared forth a recording of the national anthem, and everyone stood. But there were no speeches.

At noon on the American Legion field, I found that Lee's crossed fingers had done the trick: The barbecued beef emerged from the pits dripping juice, and so tender it crumbled from the bones. At long wooden picnic tables set up on the grass, hundreds of people ate baked beans, potato salad, and corn on the cob with their beef while old-time fiddlers, standing under a huge beach umbrella on a wagon, entertained us.

Under the broiling sun I was grateful for the surrounding views of snow-topped mountains. I remarked on the beauty of the scene to the woman beside me. But she was worried about Idaho's future. "People from California are moving in," she confided to me in a low voice, glancing furtively at the strangers at our table.

After lunch came serious business: horse racing. We cheered mightily as the sweating horses pounded around the 5/8-mile track, trailing clouds of dust that settled slowly on the spectators lining the course.

Leaving Cascade that evening, I witnessed long, slow lines of pickup campers and house trailers ascending the mountains like

Warm sun and cool water bathe "tubers" during a float on Wisconsin's Apple River. Teen-agers squeal as their inner tubes spin through white water; above, another rider whirls stiff-legged into the rapids. A church group from New London, Minnesota, links up train-style to glide along a shallow stretch of the river.

circus elephants, nose to tail. Many vehicles had boats upturned on top, or trail bikes lashed to spare tires. "Caution—Adults at Play," read a bumper sticker.

This general and determined pursuit of fun and the leisure time that permits it are rather recent developments. We inherited from our Puritan ancestors a logic that equated idleness with sinfulness. Many of the Colonies passed strict regulations "in detestation of idleness," and enforced them vigorously. As a practical matter, survival of the community demanded almost constant toil by every member, with time out only for observance of the Sabbath.

Massachusetts Bay Colony decreed that "noe idle drone bee permitted to live amongst us," and constables throughout New England sought out "all manner of gameing, singing, and dancing"— especially "Gynecandrical Dancing or that which is commonly called Mixt or Promiscuous Dancing of Men and Women." Boston refused permission for an exhibition of tightrope walking, "lest the said divertisement may tend to promote idleness in the town and great mispense of time."

"Only in this [20th] century," wrote educator Jay B. Nash, "has leisure time become something more than the Sabbath day and a few drowsy moments before sleep." He also cited a definition of recreation as "the crazy things people do to keep from going crazy," and I thought of the passage with amusement when I visited Angels Camp, California, in the Sierra Nevada foothills.

Mark Twain started it all back in 1865 when he lived for a few months in this area. He heard a tall tale in the barroom of Angels Hotel and jotted it down in his notebook: "Coleman with his jumping frog—bet a stranger $50.—Stranger had no frog and C. got him one:—In the meantime stranger filled C's frog full of shot and he couldn't jump. The stranger's frog won."

Twain converted his notes into a short story that made him famous: "The Celebrated Jumping Frog of Calaveras County." In 1928 Angels Camp staged its first Jumping Frog Jubilee to celebrate the paving of the streets. Today an elaborate four-day festival incorporates the frog contest, the county fair, a horse show, a rodeo, fireworks, band concerts, a parade, and a beauty contest.

The frog jumping competition has become an international event. The 1973 contest included entries from 18 governors and representatives of 11 foreign countries. I arrived—determined to compete—to find the town overrun with pickup campers, motorcycles, and pedestrians.

The contest takes place in a natural amphitheater, with bleachers and a grassy slope to hold the spectators. On the stage is a mat 20 feet square; toward the back of the stage, a circle the size of a dinner plate marks the spot where each frog begins his jump.

Although frog owners are warmly encouraged, they are known to be limited in number. So officials are prepared to provide frogs to competitors, and even a "jockey" for the squeamish. Each frog is permitted three jumps, and the distance is measured in a straight

Leap, frog! Hoping to startle his entry into jumping, a contestant at Angels Camp, California, takes to the air himself. A story by Mark Twain—"The Celebrated Jumping Frog of Calaveras County"—inspired the annual event. Winner in 1973: Wet Bet, with a three-jump total of 17 feet 4⅜ inches.

TOM MYERS

line from the starting point to the spot where he lands on his third jump. You may not touch your frog after he makes his first jump, but to get him started you may shout, jump up and down, tickle him, blow on him, or pound on the stage. The antics that contestants perform in attempting to persuade their frogs to jump are what the spectators come to see and applaud. Each frog must jump within 15 seconds or be disqualified. He must measure at least four inches from stem to stern. No toads are allowed.

First prize, the posters proclaimed, was $300—or $1,200 if a world record should be set. Enough people entered the 1973 contest to keep up the action for three days. Every frog had a name: I recall in particular Wounded Ankle, Croaker, Speed, Rivit, and Gorf (frog spelled backwards).

A nine-year-old boy named Matt won the Kids' Day contest with his frog, Zoom-Zoom. "I named him for a teacher, Mrs. Zumwalt," he told me. "Everybody calls her Miss Zoom-Zoom." His gaze grew distant as he perceived the possibility of future retaliation. "I hope she doesn't read the newspapers." Zoom-Zoom's distance—16 feet 1¼ inches—won Matt $15.

I approached the stage for my turn. The frogs were kept moist in wooden boxes. I plunged my arm in and pulled one out, slippery as an eel. I approached the announcer.

"My frog's name is Merrill," I told him, "for an editor who often makes *me* jump."

Merrill and I moved to the starting point—the eyes of thousands upon us—and I dropped him onto the little circle. He sat there like a handful of mud, looking sleepy. I shouted, slapped the stage, tickled him. He gave a lethargic twitch, moving perhaps four inches. I knelt behind him, hammering on the floor. At last he hurled himself across the stage, hopped again, and stopped. The tape read 4 feet 9⅛ inches. Embarrassing but not humiliating. The shortest net distance of the day was 11 inches—by a frog that gave two jumps in one direction, then a mighty leap back toward the starting point.

I carried Merrill back to his crate. He looked fully awake now and ready for a championship effort.

That night, down by the pond where the borrowed frogs are released after they've jumped, the darkness resounded to their throaty, rasping music, and I knew Merrill was among them.

Frogs croaking in the night. It is a sound we learn to live without in the city, but it can instantly summon a flood of memories of a country childhood spent around various kinds of water. I grew up in West Chester, Iowa, a village of about 200. I remember riding my bicycle along dusty gravel roads, with a gang of cronies, to an abandoned, water-filled quarry to go fishing. I doubt now that there were any fish; I have no recollection that anyone ever caught one. We didn't swim there, for horror stories from our parents—of sunken machinery and rusting coils of wire—kept us out of its spooky depths. Instead, we dived into muddy Crooked Creek, shivering as prickly crawdads brushed past our legs.

Once I won a hunting knife for catching the smallest fish in a contest at Horseshoe Pond, a mile or so outside of town, where I also tried to learn to ice-skate.

I remember making evening trips with my father and an uncle to the Skunk River to set out trotlines, and returning before dawn to check them while the river muttered ominously in the darkness and carried a layer of cold fog past our boat. And hauling in the slippery catfish. And the sun finally coming up.

In the hills above Crooked Creek, members of my family still stalk the woods in springtime, hunting the succulent morel mushrooms that grow in moist, shady spots and alongside fallen trees. Dipped in beaten eggs and flour and fried in butter, they are one of the special rewards of living in the rural Midwest. Every year, if there's a good harvest, my family sends a boxful to me in Washington, D. C. The same woods in autumn yield an abundance of hickory nuts and black walnuts, gathered under the disapproving eyes of chattering squirrels. The easy hike to collect them is a joyous way to spend a warm Sunday afternoon, surrounded by dancing leaves making their fiery farewell.

Much that rural Americans do for enjoyment is similarly low-key, informal, and spur-of-the-moment. Much of it is related to nature, to the accessibility of nature. And much of it is related to neighborliness, where people *know* their neighbors. In rural America, once in a while, there still is a barn raising, celebrated by a barn dance. Or a quilting bee. Or even a noisy, rollicking scramble for a greased pig.

And rivers, where they remain unpolluted, still lure fun-seekers. On streams as far apart as the Apple River in Wisconsin and the

Verde River in Arizona, inner-tube float trips offer a delightful way to spend a day. The course is mostly a slow one, and you drift past quiet farms in Wisconsin or through desert canyons in Arizona, past grazing cows and under highway bridges. There are enough smallish rapids to guarantee some squeals and some upsets.

Still an honored custom in rural America is the family reunion. In my own memory, reunions were always in Sunset Park, and it was always hot. There were endless varieties and quantities of food; the clank of horseshoes being pitched nearby; somebody's dog under the table; and always towering strangers exclaiming, "My, how you've grown!"

In the summer of 1973 I found myself in Alliance, Ohio, when a friend's family was about to hold a reunion, and I was invited to attend. The large, far-flung Willis family has been gathering periodically for 70 years; but nowadays every reunion is a little smaller than the last, as members move farther afield.

In a park pavilion the family conversed, compared photographs, and sat down to platters of chicken and ham, salads, beans, pies, and melons. The hat was passed to defray expenses, some of the teen-agers entertained, a short business meeting was conducted, and then there was more time for visiting before the crowd gradually dispersed for another year.

Time for visiting. A perfectly natural thing these days, I thought; but a century ago few rural Americans would have dreamed of spending a Saturday afternoon so idly. Even when the sun-to-sun work ethic began to lose its hold on farmers, as new methods and machinery gave people more free time, some still looked upon many forms of recreation with suspicion. When our ancestors found a form of idleness they enjoyed, they sometimes tried to justify it on educational grounds. Better yet was religious approval. Fishing was thus defended by an 18th-century cleric: "If I may eat them [fish] for Refreshment, I may as well catch them if this re-create and refresh me. It's as lawful to delight the Eye as the Palate."

Even circuses, as they evolved, insisted on referring to themselves as cultural and educational exhibitions, to avoid offending the sensibilities of their patrons. One advertised its menagerie as "the only moral and instructive exhibition in America."

Some superstars, of course, didn't have to advertise. One early success was Old Bet, an elephant that traveled through New England for a few years shortly after the War of 1812. Her owner, Hackaliah Bailey, to avoid providing a free show as his elephant plodded from town to town, took to traveling at night. But wily farmers lit bonfires and torches along her route, and as Old Bet trod the firelit roads, crowds gathered to roar their approval.

Circuses reached their peak of popularity in this country during the last quarter of the 19th century, when at least 40 large shows were on tour. In many rural areas they offered the only theatrical entertainment a family might see all year.

"Each year one came along from the east," wrote essayist Hamlin Garland, "trailing clouds of glorified dust and filling our minds with the color of romance. . . . it brought to our ears the latest band pieces and taught us the most popular songs. It furnished us with jokes. It relieved our dullness. It gave us something to talk about."

With the advent of movies and radio and the growing sophistication of rural audiences, the traveling circuses fell on hard times, but at least a dozen sizable shows still exist. I caught up with one in Watonga, Oklahoma, where the land is flat and fertile, with large gypsum beds under some of it, and oil rigs on top.

The five-ring Carson & Barnes Circus has toured these parts every spring, summer, and fall for 20 years, traveling some 15,000 miles annually and playing in 225 towns. The season was nearing an end when I arrived, and general manager Ted Bowman was glad. "We've been playing two shows a day, seven days a week, for eight months," he told me. "Every day in a different town, every night on the road. You have to love it to stay with it."

He didn't look any the worse for it when I found him early in the morning. Stocky, middle-aged, he radiated good health and happiness.

Why do people still come to a traveling circus, I wondered, when they can see all the acts on television?

"That's just it," Ted said. "Of course they've seen it all on TV, even the kids, but the parents remember going to the circus and loving it when they were young, and they want their children to see the real thing. There's quite a difference between an elephant on television, and having one standing five feet away from you."

It was a theme I heard over and over during the day.

"We wanted the children to see it," a parent would tell me — never quite admitting he wanted to see it himself.

On the broad fairgrounds I came to a string of 18 Indian elephants, each fastened by a rear leg to a long, stout chain. A busload of first and second graders had arrived to watch the tent go up. They watched in fascination as the elephants, munching steadily, picked up wisps of hay with their trunks.

"Where do elephants come from?" I wondered.

"Africa." "Asia."

"India?" I suggested.

"Nah."

One of the creatures turned her watery, bloodshot eyes toward us and trumpeted mightily, drawing screams of mock terror from the children. Then two of the elephants — Susie and Barbara — departed to help put up the tent, a seemingly impossible undertaking, for it was an enormous 360 feet long and 160 feet wide. "$36,000 for new canvas," Ted had told me, "every year."

Workers pounded the perimeter stakes into the ground and unrolled the canvas. One end was lifted, men and elephants disappeared under it, and the animals' harnesses were attached through pulleys to the poles. At a signal they lumbered forward, trumpeting, and the great poles went up with surprising ease. A gust of wind found its way under the canvas and it seemed to breathe. Steadily it rose as the elephants pulled. Suddenly the big top was in place, pennants flapping gaily.

A menagerie outside the main tent attracted comment as the crowd gathered. "See how well he chews his food," said a mother pointedly to her young son as they stood in front of the camel's pen.

The performances—at 3 p.m. and 8:30—went off smoothly. The afternoon audience wasn't very large, but in the evening nearly every seat was filled.

Clowns and jugglers, tightrope walkers and lion tamer, trapeze acts and animal acts—in the excitement time passed quickly, and too soon it was over. Filing out, the crowd seemed happy—except for one small boy whose balloon got away from him and sailed slowly to the very top of the tent.

State and county fairs have some of the entertainment trappings of traveling carnivals and circus sideshows. But their real purpose is quite different—for they are both educational exhibits and showcases for the farmer's and homemaker's arts. Many innovations in agricultural methods and machinery are introduced at fairs. Farm families have traditionally looked forward eagerly to the yearly gathering, the excitement of the crowds and special events, the chance to enter the farm's choicest products in competition, perhaps to win a blue ribbon.

The custom of market fairs, sometimes with horse racing and other diversions, came to America from Europe during the colonial period. But the first modern fairs, with their emphasis on "agricultural improvement," were sponsored by Elkanah Watson and the Berkshire Agricultural Society early in the 19th century. By 1868 there were more than 1,300 agricultural societies, most of which held annual fairs. In 1972 more than 70 million Americans spent $200 million at 2,150 state and county fairs.

One hot August day I stopped at the Winnebago County Fair in Pecatonica, Illinois—in America's breadbasket. It had been years since I had attended such an event, but the sights, sounds, and smells were all familiar: the tinny music of the midway, the sizzling hot dogs, the long, hushed halls filled with tables of preserves and flower arrangements, walls of quilts and artwork, the winning entries festooned with ribbons.

Over the public-address system came personal messages:

"Ron Zimmerman, please move your truck."

"Bob McCulloch, your family's waiting for you at the south gate."

The tractor pulling contest astonished me: roaring behemoths dragging tons of dead weight, spewing smoke, trailing clouds of dust a hundred yards behind.

Resting my aching feet, I sat on hard wooden bleachers as Holsteins paraded around a judging ring, their anxious owners prodding and tugging at them as though they were oversized entrants at a dog show. Clarence Moore, the young judge, scrutinized the creatures like a critical shopper, ranking them finally in a line. Despite a broken arm and badly bruised leg, the results of an encounter with an unbroken pony two days before, he put in a long day. As the cattle passed from the ring he would comment on them for the audience, *(Continued on page 140)*

Family reunion brings all ages to a park pavilion in Alliance, Ohio, for a nostalgic get-together and a bountiful home-cooked dinner. The Willises have gathered every summer for 70 years as the family has grown and prospered. Mr. and Mrs. Victor Willis (opposite, below) pause in their melon-slicing chores to greet a grandson and namesake, Victor Smith. Below, Elizabeth Willis (in print dress) and Erma Willis compare snapshots. Meanwhile Matthew Hannen (opposite) gets his face washed after eating. The Ohio Willises descend from "Old John" Willis, a native Pennsylvanian who married three times and fathered 17 children. Like many rural families, the Willises find their reunions attracting fewer and fewer numbers as children marry and scatter across the country.

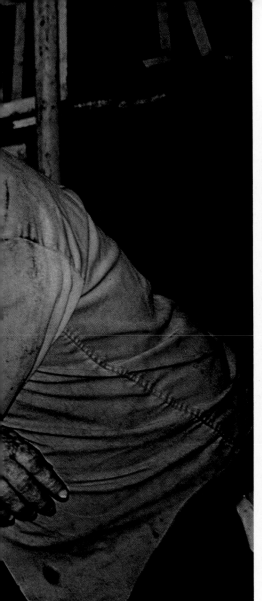

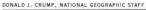

Costumed dog named Pierre awaits his cue with a weary roustabout behind the center ring of the Carson & Barnes Circus during a performance in Watonga, Oklahoma. The dog will soon entertain the crowd, and the workman will help pack the troupe for the move to another town—one of 225 stops in the company's grueling, two-shows-a-day tour. For many Americans the big top evokes memories of a rural childhood, when circus-day excitement began before dawn. Youngsters still find many of the attractions their parents remember, including cotton candy and trumpeting elephants. A busload of Watonga schoolchildren arrives as the elephants eat. Later two of the animals helped raise the tent.

mentioning one cow's "upstandingness," another's "little more depth of rib" or "sharpness and cleanness up through the front end"; he liked another because she "holds together well" and had "a little more dairyness."

Holder of a Ph.D. in animal science from South Dakota State University at Brookings, Moore served for two years with the Agricultural Extension Service in Hawaii before joining the faculty of Illinois State University in 1961. There he has taught and been in charge of the dairy herd, except during a six-month sabbatical leave in New Zealand.

He started judging livestock as a 4-H club member, he told me, and then entered intercollegiate competition as a member of the South Dakota State stockjudging team. "Now it's more or less a summertime hobby for me," he said.

I expressed some doubt that a man could look at hundreds of cows during the course of a day and remain clearheaded enough to pick the best from each group. "Well," he said, "I carry the image of an ideal cow in my head, and I just compare it with every animal that comes into the ring. You don't get tired of looking at something beautiful."

"How much bearing does the way an animal is shown have on the results?" I asked.

"Well, a good showman can conceal certain faults in a cow and cover up some defects by keeping the animal moving and looking alert, or posed properly when it's standing. How the animal is trained and fitted—its general condition, how its hair is clipped, its feet trimmed, and how clean it is — are also important. Of course, we judge the animal, not the showman, but it can make a difference. We have special showmanship classes for young boys and girls so they can learn the art of fitting and showing an animal."

And just what is "dairyness"?

"Milking ability," he said. "Sharp, angular lines, clean throughout, free from coarseness. We want a cow that will return a profit for its owner, not just this year but for years to come."

Later I wandered into the cattle barn, a cool, humid enclosure filled with breezes from electric fans and muted music from transistor radios. Cows reclined—chewing, always chewing—their legs tucked under them, their tails swishing. Sparrows chirped in the rafters overhead, and young men in T-shirts rearranged beds of straw with pitchforks. Across the tops of the stalls, rosette prize ribbons bloomed like chrysanthemums. There were bulls in that barn bigger than my kitchen.

Watching over a dozen Holstein dairy cows was Laurie Thomson, looking far too young, I thought, for such a responsibility.

"Are all these cows yours?" I asked, expecting her to say, "No, they're my father's."

"Yes," she said. She and her husband, Jim, have about 120 head of dairy cattle on a farm near Utica, Illinois. In the summer, Laurie shows the cattle while her husband minds the farm.

Do the cows like going to fairs?

"They don't mind," Laurie laughed. "They're so used to it. They

Retired rancher Horace J. Patterson rests his horse, Lady, as the Thunder Mountain Days parade forms in Cascade, Idaho. Now 79, Patterson has ridden in the July 4 procession every year since 1938.

go where we take them. We were at the Boone County Fair last week. Tomorrow we'll take them home, and the week after next we go to the Mendota Fair.''

I asked her to point out to me, with the help of one of her prize-winners, what makes a good Holstein. ''Well,'' she said, approaching a beautiful black-and-white animal, ''she should be tall, and flat on top, like this, and not bulgy here'' — in the shoulders — ''and she has to have good legs. And a good udder, of course.''

Was Dr. Moore a good judge?

''Oh, yes. Very good,'' she said. ''Especially after a few that we've had lately.''

We went outside to where Borba, her 2,400-pound, prize-winning bull was penned.

''He's the best bull of all the dairy breeds,'' she said. ''It's the fourth year he's won it.'' Borba seemed indifferent to our presence. ''He's about as quiet a bull as you could get,'' Laurie said. ''No temper.'' She explained the point system whereby animals are rated: Good, Very Good, Excellent. ''Borba got Very Good,'' she said. ''He would have got Excellent but his legs are too straight. *Too straight!* We're just sick about it.''

If a dairy cow possesses dairyness, does a work mule possess workness, or just cussedness, I wondered as I later attended the Tennessee State Fair in Nashville. Sweating owners manhandled the balky creatures — hee-hawing, wheezing like broken engines —

around the ring. They were beautiful animals, the color of rich caramel, with incredibly large, mobile ears that they swiveled like antennae.

When I had watched the mules for a while, I stopped by the pavilion where the Methodist ladies were serving lunch: white beans with ham over corn bread, with onions and relish sprinkled on top. After eating I strolled through the grounds and the midway, with its throngs of people, paused with them uneasily at a glass cage full of wriggling rattlesnakes, had my weight and age guessed (quite accurately), and saw roosters with mad, feverish eyes scratching angrily in their cages in the poultry barn. I followed along behind a 4-H group as they competed in judging contests, exchanging impassive stares with truculent pigs and sleepy steers. I watched a big black Angus bull getting a hose bath — flattening his ears to keep the water out, lifting his head for a neck wash, shuddering when the cold water hit a tender spot, squinting into the spray, a disgruntled frown on his face.

Toward the end of the day I won a stuffed donkey at the bingo tent, and went home highly pleased with myself.

The circus, medicine shows, fairs, tent chautauquas — these provided highlights of the year for our rural forebears. The traveling chautauquas and the medicine shows are long gone; the circus hangs on; only the fairs seem to get bigger. But not necessarily better. I can remember a trip to the Iowa State Fair in Des Moines when I was very young. I fell asleep during the evening grandstand show, finally to be roused by the fireworks: a gloriously exciting way for a small boy to awaken, to find the sky filled with fire and noise.

The chautauquas were before my time, although I remember my parents talking about them. Named for the lake in western New York where it got its start, the Chautauqua Institution in 1874 began presenting summer cultural programs: religion, education, music, art, and drama.

In 1904, traveling units began to bring such programs to rural America. In those days before radio, when a tent chautauqua came to town for a week the populace of the area made an extended picnic of the occasion, playing baseball and croquet during the day and attending lectures and concerts in the afternoons and evenings. A program for a typical Chautauqua Week in 1920 in Milford, Iowa, boasted the New York Glee Club; Lou J. Beauchamp, The Laughing Philosopher; lectures on "The Indispensable Tools of Democracy" and "The Call of the Hour"; an impersonator of "the world's most interesting characters," and a six-piece orchestra, "rendering gems from the symphony classics." With such lecturers as William Jennings Bryan, James Whitcomb Riley, Horace Greeley, P. T. Barnum, and Mark Twain, traveling chautauquas brought a taste of glamor and reflected fame to many a rural area.

The residents of nearly every rural region in America will defend theirs as the most beautiful, most productive, friendliest, or generally grandest area on the continent — and push the claim with an annual festival of some sort. There are music festivals and historical observances, square-dance contests and old-home days, strawberry festivals and corn festivals, festivals for watermelons, cotton, tobacco, peaches, roses, locust blossoms, and crawfish.

In Canton, Texas, population 2,283, a custom that began a century ago continues to lure crowds. The three-day event called First Monday—held each month on the first Monday and preceding weekend—celebrates the rural American's bartering instincts. In 1973 a ten-day centennial observance drew some 200,000 people to barter or sell furniture, guns, antiques, coon dogs, player pianos, freshly-caught catfish, and just about anything else you can think of. Apparently many people make a hobby of traveling around Texas or beyond to attend such trading days.

Hobbies are as important to rural Americans as anyone else, perhaps more so. Farther from the diversions and distractions of city life, they tend to rely upon their own devices for amusement. I journeyed deep into Mississippi to meet some coon hunters, men whose hobby is as old as the country itself. The little town of Leakesville was all astir, for only a couple of weeks before, two men who had been fishing on the Pascagoula River claimed to have been taken for a ride in a strange machine, an "unidentified flying object."

"It's interesting, trying to figure out that UFO business," said Judge Darwin M. Maples as we talked in his chambers. "But to tell the truth, I'd rather be out with my dogs."

Judge Maples, an experienced coon hunter, defends the sport vigorously. "I don't believe I've ever had a coon hunter in my court," he said. "It's a nice solitary sport, something you can do by yourself, whenever you want, on a moment's notice. You can walk 30 minutes in any direction from here and be in coon hunting country. And there's more to it than you might think. Coons are smart. They'll trick a young dog—make him think they've gone up a tree while they keep on running."

If the coons are smart, so—by necessity—are the dogs and the men who train them. A toothless old gentleman, nearly crippled by rheumatism and described by a friend as "the biggest liar in nine states," told me of being approached by a man who wanted some help in training a bulldog. "I says to 'im, 'Well, the first thing, Charlie,' I says, 'is you got to have more sense than the dang dog.'"

Barry Wallace, a lanky young county agricultural extension agent with a drawl as slow and warm as the South, has a living room filled with trophies won by his dogs in tracking competitions. He consented to take me along on a hunt; so that night we loaded a couple of his dogs—Ol' Preacher and a puppy—into the back of his pickup, and joined Laverne Landrum and his dog Squeller (pronounced squealer). Through the dark night we drove to a cornfield surrounded by woods. Once out of the truck, the dogs yapped and strained at their leashes. "Hush up," Barry said to them. They ignored him. "Might as well tell a dead man to roll over."

Cars, campers, and trucks jam the city park in Canton, Texas, for First Monday—a time of trading and selling. From all over the country antique dealers and collectors arrive for the monthly event. In 1973—First Monday's centennial year—200,000 people descended on the little town for a special ten-day celebration that included Labor Day weekend. They exchanged everything from shotguns to hunting dogs, phonograph records to player pianos. Surrounded by clutter, a dealer (opposite) waits for customers. Another participant roams the grounds with a pet raccoon clinging to his shoulder.

Gillette

Turned loose, the dogs scurried off, their wagging tails rustling the dry corn. We stood and listened. The still, cold night resounded to the sound of distant house dogs exchanging barks. There was a noise in the brush: an armadillo, Barry said. Presently we heard one of our dogs. "That's just the puppy, barkin' at the fence." Later there was a bark from Ol' Preacher.

"Hear that?" said Barry to Laverne. "Where's that dog of yours?"

"He's there. He knows your dog's lyin'."

"Preachers don't lie."

As we began walking through the dark woods toward the sound of the barking, our way lit by the lamps worn miner-like on Barry and Laverne's hard hats, the two men kept up a running, good-natured debate over the relative merits of their dogs. Squeller was barking now. "That dog of Barry's is what you call a semi-silent trailer," said Laverne. "Highly undesirable."

"Squeller probably got his nose in an old armadillo hole," said Barry. "If he don't hurry up, the *puppy's* gonna show him where that coon went."

All three dogs had now stopped, and there was a new note to their barking that signaled they had treed a coon. "A hunter who knows his hound can tell what's happening," Barry explained. "The tone tells when it's trailing in water, or on dry land, or how fresh the scent is. The song of the hounds tells a story."

The distant chorus hung in the still air like smoke. The woods smelled clean and fresh, and the night-time chill crept through our heavy coats. I could almost feel the darkness. Our route dipped downward and the ground became soggy, then wet, as we went deeper into a swamp. The moon made ghosts of dangling Spanish moss. Soon we were up to our ankles in black water and muck. I began to wonder about the alligators and snakes that reportedly infested these woods, and remembered the wild hog we had come upon earlier while driving through the swamp. He stood defiantly in the middle of the road, snorting angrily, his hackles bristling along his back.

Then we came upon the dogs, gathered around a huge cypress, hurling themselves at the trunk, making a dreadful din. Using "squallers"—little wooden trumpets similar to duck callers—Barry and Laverne imitated the sound of enraged, snarling coons, and from the branches high overhead three pairs of bright eyes peered down into the light of the lamps.

At night, coons can only be seen in the treetops when light from below is reflected in their eyes, and either from instinct or lack of interest they usually refuse to look down until the noise of the squallers arouses their fatal curiosity.

Barry shot one "so the puppy will know what he's been chasing. I only kill a coon if I'm training a dog. Otherwise he doesn't under-stand. Meat and hide hunters can take a good dog and wipe out an area's coon population in just a little while. We work hard here to conserve our game. We plant food crops for them, and never take more than one per hunt." In field competitions, where Barry spends most of his weekends, the coons are never harmed.

Eager for the hunt, coonhounds tug at leashes held by owner Barry Wallace of Leakesville, Mississippi. In field competitions dogs score on their ability to strike a scent, then trail and tree a raccoon.

Fall weekends bring another favorite diversion to many an American small town: the high school football game. Townspeople often follow the team's fortunes with an intense civic interest reserved in cities for college or professional teams.

"The bruising of shins," wrote diarist William Bentley of a game akin to modern football played in Massachusetts late in the 1700's, "has rendered it rather disgraceful to those of better education, who use a hand ball, thrown up against an house or fence instead of the Foot Ball, which is unfriendly to clothes, as well as safety."

Clothes and safety can still take a beating, especially in those parts of the country where high school football is a serious business. I watched a game in Elizabethville, Pennsylvania, with the cold wind of November whistling under the bleachers alongside the Upper Dauphin Area field, and remembered how exciting a good high school game can be.

Coach Tom Hain's Trojans were undefeated in 20 straight games, and had lost only six in five years. They were finishing their season with Homecoming against their arch rivals, the Millersburg Indians. The Trojans had had only 20 points scored against them all year, while averaging 46 against their opponents. High school football in Elizabethville has some of the trappings of the college sport: game films, expensive equipment, a four-man coaching staff, a press box above the bleachers.

"We get a lot of support from the parents," Tom told me before the game. "The Football Fathers Club raised $16,000 a couple of years ago to install the lights and build the refreshment stand and press box."

In the locker room, as the players suited up, I was struck by their youth; I was certain I couldn't have been that young when I was in high school. Their long winning streak and the school's winning tradition had made them confident. "They're so confident," said Tom, "that when they go out to play a game they just act like they're going to work."

Head coach for five years, an alumnus of Elizabethville himself, Tom understood what made the boys try so hard. "Pride," he said. "They're proud to be winners. They know what they have to do, and they just go out and do it."

They did it to Millersburg, winning 26-6 before 2,760 shivering fans. The game was looser and in ways more exciting than many professional games I've seen, with fumbles picked up and run for touchdowns, blocked kicks, long runs, wild passes somehow caught, and razzle-dazzle plays. The Trojans' first play from scrimmage, for instance, was the famous old Statue of Liberty, and it gained 20 yards.

The fans were like a Super Bowl crowd, screaming themselves hoarse and throwing confetti. Both bands performed at half time, the home ensemble including in their repertoire the theme music from television's Masterpiece Theater in a routine complete with majorettes in miniskirts marching with wooden rifles.

After the game, everybody—including the band director—got thrown in the shower.

Pride is the motivation, too, for ethnic, civic, and religious groups who stage observances honoring some common tie. Often these are colorful events that evoke memories of a homeland two or three generations removed. A large group of Mennonites, from Germany by way of Russia, settled near Freeman, South Dakota, in 1874. Every year they stage a grand banquet called Schmeckfest, or "tasting festival," and serve traditional European foods to thousands of people.

The highways here run straight to the horizon, and you feel like an arrow hurtling along them. Starlings perched on telephone lines peel off as if choreographed as you drive by. This is hunting country, and a taxidermist advertises his trade with a signboard showing a pheasant in flight. The self-serve laundry posts a sign asking patrons to empty their pockets, please, of coins, bolts, and bullets.

The Freeman Junior College Women's Auxiliary sponsors the Schmeckfest, turning the profits over to the school. I took this year's co-chairwomen—Mrs. LeRoy Hofer and Mrs. Lemoyne Ries—away from their busy kitchen in the college cafeteria to ask them about the event.

"This is our 15th year," said Mrs. Hofer, "and the first time we've made it a three-day affair. The first one—a single night—taught us a lesson: We didn't have an advance ticket sale, and hundreds of people showed up and stood in line for hours, and many didn't get anything to eat!"

"It's a tremendous lot of work," said Mrs. Ries. "It takes weeks of preparation, and the women are on their feet in the kitchen from early morning until well after dark. We'll feed about a thousand guests a night, plus 200 waitresses, cooks, and other workers. But we love doing it. And everyone helps. The older ladies wrap silverware, for instance, and the appliance man loans us a drier for the dish towels. Lots of the townspeople help that way."

Mrs. Hofer listed for me some of the ingredients that were going into the preparation of the meals over the three days: 1,425 pounds of stewing beef, 1,000 pounds of potatoes, 67 pounds of coffee, 81 gallons of sauerkraut, 225 hens for broth, six boxes of toothpicks.

Though the serving wasn't to begin until 4 that afternoon, by 10 a.m. the kitchen was already emitting delicious odors. I dashed through the steadily falling rain to an adjacent building where cooking and crafts were being demonstrated, and baked goods, preserves, and handicraft products sold. Several women were making noodles, taffy, and bratwurst. Others demonstrated the use of a mangle iron and the spinning of yarn.

Two busloads of tourists from the Adventurers' Travel Club in Sioux City, Iowa, trooped through, staying carefully in line, snapping up bargains and loaves of bread. I was told that people come to Schmeckfest from as far away as Illinois and Texas.

Later I sat down to a table straining under the weight of noodle soup, green-bean soup, stewed beef (*Dampffleisch*), German fried potatoes, sauerkraut, bratwurst, creamed peas and carrots, salads, buns, rolls, loaf breads, coffee cake, and various undefined pastries and delicacies.

Across from me was a nervous young high school student—his mother carefully supervising his eating—who was to appear later in the chorus of a production of "Oklahoma!" in the auditorium. Beside me was a very elderly lady, nearly deaf, whose bright eyes nevertheless took in everything.

There was a steady hum of conversation, occasionally swelling to a roar, punctuated by bursts of laughter and the clatter of silverware. I ate as much as I possibly could, and leaned back reflecting on all the labor that had gone into the Schmeckfest, and the will that would keep the people of Freeman working long into the night to ensure their guests an enjoyable experience.

The pursuit of happiness, we were told long ago, is one of our inalienable rights; but were these people simply pursuing happiness, or something more elusive? Was it the *sharing* of happiness, perhaps?

The old lady turned to me. "Isn't it nice," she said, her voice whispery with age, her thin hand as light as a tiny bird on my wrist. "Isn't it nice to see people you love having a good time?"

Yes. It is.

Outside, the rain had stopped, and stars glittered in parking lot puddles. From the auditorium came the first tentative sounds of the orchestra, tuning up.

Sugar-dipped pastry clings to the face of Michael Regier at a cooking demonstration staged during a three-day Schmeckfest — or "tasting festival" — in Freeman, South Dakota. Each year Mennonite women of the little farming community serve dinners prepared with recipes inherited from previous generations. At the 1973 event, 3,000 diners sat down to tables crowded with such dishes as green-bean soup with summer savory and sour cream, and Dampffleisch — stewed beef.

Shadows of evening darken the walls of Mount Olive Baptist Church, a sturdy brick structure

Chapter Five

School, club, congregation:
"The fellowship of kindred minds"

crowning a hilltop near Salem, West Virginia. On Sunday mornings worshipers fill the pews.

153

By Stratford C. Jones

Hands clasped in the hands of those beside us, we sat around the laden table. To a tune from *Johnny Appleseed* we sang grace, ending with the words, "The Lord's been good to me." And indeed He had, murmured Leon Neher as he looked at the open, healthy faces of his family, smelled the hot wheat muffins, baked chicken, salad, and corn—all "home-grown"—and thought of the condition of the farm and the character of friends and neighbors.

Leon, 39, his wife, Linda, and their four children join his town-dwelling parents in operating a 1,200-acre farm just outside Quinter, a town of 900 in northwestern Kansas. Grain elevators tower above the tree-shaded streets, but grain no longer dominates the area's economy; beef, hog, and dairy operations and the manufacture of farm equipment are now important contributors.

Leon, whose sharp features and jawline fringe of beard give him a look both shrewd and quizzical, was born and reared in Quinter. He went away to college in the early 1950's, did graduate work in sociology and theology, and then taught at Manchester College in Indiana.

Four years ago he returned to the farm. He continues to teach—at Colby Community College—but he now considers himself primarily a farmer. The reasons for the move largely have to do with his family: opportunities for his youngsters to "learn more than how to carry out the garbage," and benefits of living close to grandparents and other relatives.

During my visit with the Nehers we talked at length about differences between urban and rural life. In urban areas, we agreed, personal and social relationships often revolve around business and government; in rural America the most important institutions are still the family, school, church, and community organizations. But Leon cautioned against too-sweeping generalizations. "You know, one of the great myths is that rural America is religious," he said. "That's not necessarily so."

The Nehers belong to Quinter's Church of the Brethren, and Leon is on the national board of that denomination. The town also has five other churches: the Dunkard Brethren, Old Order German Baptist Brethren, Reformed Presbyterian, United Methodist, and an independent congregation that calls its premises His Place. "Still, I'll bet that on any one Sunday no more than a fourth of this community will be in church," Leon said.

Nevertheless, I believe there is a greater awareness of the churches in rural areas than elsewhere and, conversely, that they have greater influence there. One reason is that rural churches often are main centers of social activity; another is that in places of small population, the church leaders are known personally to almost everybody.

Next morning, in the rain, I set off for an appointment with Ormond Breeden at Quinter High School. A compact man with strong hands and pale blue eyes, he has taught vocational agriculture there for 24 years.

In the past, many of Quinter High's students planned to spend their lives on farms. But that's no longer the case, Ormond told me as we talked in the shop of the two-story, tan brick building.

"The 'vo-ag' curriculum is changing," he explained. "With the cost of land and machinery going up, and the need for manpower going down, opportunities for getting into farming are limited. So now I teach more courses like agribusiness—with on-the-job training in the feed mill in town—and agri-industry, with training in the tillage-tools factory." Girls now take his courses, too.

Most youths specifically preparing to become farmers get a major share of their training the most practical way of all: working on a farm and participating in such organizations as a 4-H club or Future Farmers of America. During my visit the Neher children —Tom, 13, Debbie, 11, and Mike, 10—won 23 ribbons at a 4-H fair. Mark, 2, wasn't quite ready to compete.

On the eve of the livestock competition, the youngsters hosed down their hogs and scrubbed them with stiff brushes. Next day they finished "prettying them up," dusting the white ones with baby powder and shining the reddish ones with liberal applications of furniture polish, an approved cosmetic for hogs. The ribbons they brought home indicated all the extra effort was worthwhile; but Tom took pains to assure me that the important thing was the basic soundness of the animals, resulting from breeding and the right care and feeding.

The Nehers and I had talked about the importance of organizations in small towns, and Quinter itself is a good illustration. While the men have contented themselves with Kiwanis and Rotary, the women over the years have formed seven federated women's clubs—nationally affiliated groups dedicated to topical discussions and self-improvement—and more than 20 social clubs, one with a men's auxiliary that plays cards while the women sew.

Ura Jamison, a sprightly widow with a shy smile, is a member of Quinter's oldest federated club, Minerva. She lives on a farm but now cooks two days a week at a restaurant in town. After work one afternoon we sat in a booth and talked.

"I also belong to the second oldest social club in town, P.A.L.," she said. "Started that in 1926." Laughing heartily, she confided that the initials stood for "Peppy Aproned Ladies."

"Now you be sure to put down that we don't gossip," she said with a shake of her finger. "We just meet once a month and exchange all kinds of information.

"All but one of us are grandmothers, and five are great-grandmothers, and that makes for a lot to talk about. We reminisce a lot, too, because we've had some good times over the years. Oh, you bet we have!"

On that visit to the plains of Kansas, and later in Montana and Arkansas and elsewhere as I traveled through rural America, my affection for country life was rekindled. The assignment stirred memories of the 1940's when I spent four years on my grandparents' farm on the Gaspé Peninsula of eastern Canada. Wood fueled our stove, kerosene our lamps, *(Continued on page 160)*

Seldom glancing at the Gospel he has preached for 20 years, the Reverend John Finn—known to parishioners as Brother John—delivers a sermon at the First Baptist Church of Jasper, Arkansas. "Although I quote from memory, I find people listen better to a preacher with the Good Book open before him," Mr. Finn says. His wife, Bette, below in dark blue, sings beside their son, Rodney, at vacation Bible school graduation exercises in Omaha, Arkansas. Mr. Finn opened the program with pledges of allegiance to the flag and to the Bible.

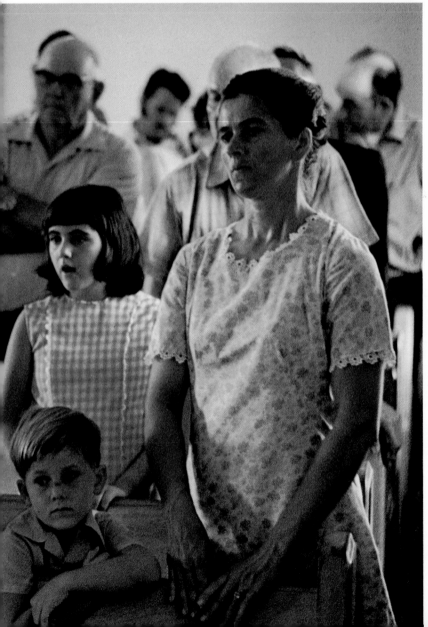

Wading toward a pebbled bank of the Buffalo River, the Reverend Herman Ballentine of St. Joe, Arkansas, and three youngsters he has just baptized link hands in new fellowship as members of the Baptist Church. John Finn, the guest preacher, offers a prayer of thanks for those "who have experienced salvation and have obeyed Christ by being baptized." Mr. Ballentine, waist-deep in water, performed the ordinance of baptism by immersing each child. The barefoot boys, hair toweled dry, bow their heads in a closing prayer with their families and friends. Besides assisting at baptisms and conducting vacation Bible schools, Mr. Finn helps other Baptist ministers organize revivals, substitutes for ill or vacationing preachers, and aids in finding new clergymen for congregations that need them. He also roams the backwoods of the Ozark Mountains, knocking at unfamiliar doors and delivering Christ's message to anyone who will listen.

NATHAN BENN

Row of signs along Interstate 70 tells motorists of the choice of churches in Quinter, Kansas, a town of 900.

and hay the horses that were our only means of transport.

Because church lay nine miles away by road and ferry—a bit closer when we could drive a sleigh across the frozen Restigouche River—we did most of our praying at home. There, too, I did my schoolwork, tutored by my mother, who had first taught in a one-room school at the age of 17. There was a small school about two miles away, but the snowdrifts that sometimes reached roof level were sufficient obstacle when I had a qualified teacher at home.

Weather and distance still force special arrangements for the education of youngsters living in remote spots. A friend who ranches in Wyoming tells me that his wife and daughters now rent a house in town during the winter to be near the high school, while he and his eighth-grade son remain on the ranch. In southeastern Oregon, the Crane Union High School District has been providing boarding facilities for students since the 1920's.

Of the 84 students in the huge district—approximately the size of New Jersey—73 share a new dormitory and dining room financed by tax revenues that otherwise would pay for bus transportation. Several of the boarders live more than a hundred miles from the school; in one case, 136 miles.

The school's one bus, with 36 reclining seats, is used for student-activity trips that average 180 miles each way. Some of the football team's opponents are more than 250 miles distant.

I stayed two nights at the dormitory, eating and talking with the students, almost all ranchers' children and almost all well-adjusted to their situation. Said student body president Phil Davis, a rugged blond cowboy of 17, "Here you're on your own, making a lot of your own decisions, because your parents are so far away."

John Robinson, a former school superintendent who captains a commercial fishing boat in summer, bunks on the lower floor with the boys while his wife, Bertha, lives upstairs with the girls. Three out of five of the students continue their education after graduation, Robinson said. "They have a high rate of survival in college. They're self-sufficient and already oriented toward dorm life."

Not more than a generation ago, many a farm district's school schedule was tailored to the harvest season. In Maine's potato country, that is still true. Several of Aroostook County's school

systems adjust their calendars so children can be available when needed and still get a full year's education. In mid-August, when school opens in Monticello, Maine, just west of the Canadian border, the district's million-dollar crop of potatoes lies buried in fields green with leafy plants. A month later, when the crop is ready for harvest, classes stop for three weeks while the children work for their parents or other growers, collecting the machine-dug potatoes in baskets and emptying them into barrels.

I was tardy by a couple of minutes on opening day, and the fourth-grade teacher, Mrs. Margaret Hoyt, motioned me to a table at the back of the room. My seat was beside a window overlooking a meadow backed by pines. There, one of my classmates told me at recess, a moose sometimes browses.

We did a lot that first day, recounting summer fun but also getting into such solid subjects as addition and cursive writing. I did so poorly in the latter that Mrs. Hoyt felt obliged to pass my paper around as an example of "how busy adults write."

Monticello's fourth graders and I still correspond. John Britton, for instance, tells me he has my infamous writing sample fixed to his bedroom wall, and Leslie Smith sends word he earned $59 at harvest time.

Near Monticello School stands a silver-gray Grange Hall, a symbol of the community's agricultural heritage. More than 600,000 persons in 41 states belong to the Grange, a fraternal and cooperative association formed in 1867 to encourage farmers to meet, talk, buy, and act together. Perhaps most important, the Grange meetings then as now provided farm families with opportunities to socialize.

Wendell Harvey, the Monticello Grangemaster, was awaiting his turn at bat in a softball game behind the hall. "When I joined the Grange here in 1968, membership was down to about 40," he said. "But it's been picking up, and now we have 108 on the books. We've got a young bunch, and not all are farmers. For example, I'm a maintenance supervisor at a shopping center in Houlton."

Dorothy Wood joined the Monticello Grange way back in 1914. "Why, before the coming of the *(Continued on page 169)*

Concrete silos of a grain storage elevator loom above Quinter on the Kansas plains. At the dinner table, Leon Neher and his family join in prayer. In 1969 sociologist Neher returned to Quinter, his birthplace, to become a partner in his father's farm. "I felt the family would benefit from my being in an occupation in which they could be involved," he says. Below, seated visitors chat with members at a meeting of one of Quinter's women's clubs.

LINDA BARTLETT (OPPOSITE AND BELOW)

With a sure hand, Juliette Michelle Burke outlines an Easter picture during Sunday school in Willis Chapel at Huntly, Virginia. Above, white-robed children of the United Methodist Church youth choir in nearby Sperryville lift their voices in an Easter anthem: "Jerusalem, Jerusalem! Sing for the night is o'er!" After the morning service, youngsters linger in the warmth of spring.

automobile, the Grange was the center of activity in places like this," she said. Mrs. Wood and her husband, Charles, a retired agriculture teacher, now live in Houlton and attend Grange meetings in both towns. But, said Mr. Wood, they no longer hold office: "You gradually break away after several hundred years and let somebody else do the work."

Esau Jenkins started life as a laborer, then turned to truck farming on the loamy soil of Johns Island on the South Carolina coast. Poor black families comprise almost half the population of the 74-square-mile island, some of which lies so low even shallow graves must be bailed by bucket before the dead can be lowered to rest. Eventually Jenkins became a businessman and established a local bus and trucking service, but it is for his achievements as a community leader that he is remembered. His efforts brought the island a consumers' cooperative, a credit union, a high school, and adult education courses. He died in an automobile accident only a few months before I visited the island.

"When Papa died, it was like a part of the island sank under," said his son, Abraham, 44, a retired Air Force navigator who now serves as administrator of the island's health clinic.

Esau Jenkins left Johns Islanders a legacy of literacy and political effectiveness. In 1948, as a bus owner, he was driving neighbors to jobs in Charleston and decided they could spend their time en route learning to read, at least enough to pass the test that was then a state requirement for voter registration.

"Then the bus people and friends formed a little club, with Papa as president," Abraham Jenkins recalled. "They named it the Progressive Club. Papa borrowed money to put up a big concrete-block building that contained the first gymnasium on the island, and they began to hold all kinds of classes there.

"Papa used the church, too, just like a preacher," Abraham said. "Everybody else would go up there and talk about heaven and hell, but he'd be up there talking about better citizenship."

Next morning I stood in a side door of that church—Wesley United Methodist—and watched the Reverend Willis T. Goodwin walk toward me from his house down Bohicket Road. The 6-foot-3-inch minister stopped several times to talk with youngsters, clasping a hand, patting a shoulder.

Eventually my turn came; we shook hands and entered the cluttered, book-lined office from where he wrestles with the needs of 2,500 parishioners.

"In black rural America, everything is centered on the church," said Dr. Goodwin, paster of five congregations on South Carolina's Sea Islands. "The church *is* the community organization, and when it fails to organize well, it fails its people.

On an early-spring visit to their family plot, a father and son pause at a grave on the grounds of the Jerusalem United Methodist Church at Warrenton, North Carolina. The cemetery dates from the 1840's.

"Historically, country blacks looked to the church. They figured the preacher knew everything. Often he was the only one who could read, and even today they assume he must know how to get things done. If a person needs his house repaired, he comes to the church, not the government, and the church contacts the government agencies because it's all too bewildering for most people.

"Another thing," Dr. Goodwin said. "The church has been the only place blacks could express themselves. They couldn't go to local government and sound off, so they went to church where they could testify and shout. The only thing in rural America that blacks can feel a part of is the church. That's the way it used to be, and lots of places that's the way it still is."

For rural southwesterners of Spanish and Mexican descent, religion has played a somewhat similar sustaining role. At Polvadera, New Mexico, the most important event of the year is the feast of San Lorenzo, the town's patron saint. In the pure, fading desert light of an August evening, I joined a small group of men conversing in Spanish on the stone terrace of the pink stucco church. Most wore boots, freshly laundered trousers, and colorful shirts. One, a short, trim man with graying hair, had just driven in from California; Fred Chavez told me he was one of many reared in Polvadera who try to make an annual pilgrimage to the celebration from other parts of the country.

As the hour arrived, we slipped inside the church and ranged along the rear wall. Women and children, quietly fanning themselves, already filled the two ranks of pine pews. The Reverend Laurier A. Labreche, wavy dark hair glistening, intoned the liturgy of the Mass. When the service ended, the members of the congregation stood and turned to greet one another; a long-haired youth in a shimmering blue shirt on my right and a cowboy on my left exchanged handshakes with me, and we filed out into the indigo night. There we divided into two columns and marched in procession around the dusty churchyard, with two couples bearing aloft the small image of San Lorenzo, visible to all beneath the waxing moon.

Several hundred yards away, in what seemed a different world, the silhouettes of tractor-trailers raced by on Interstate 25, their roar overcome by our voices raised in the refrain of *Jesus Mi Amor*.

Next day at Zuni, New Mexico, I talked with the Reverend Meldon Hickey, who had recently taken over as director of the St. Anthony Indian Mission. The soft-spoken Franciscan is no newcomer to this work, however; he has headed other missions nearby in his 21 years with the Pueblo tribes. At 49, his thinning hair is almost white, but his face is still young.

"The Zuni religion is very demanding," Father Meldon said. "The people have very little time left over for Catholicism."

Some, however, do take time for both. When I asked why, the priest replied: "As one of them once said, a wagon being pulled by one horse will probably reach its destination, but how much better the chance if two are pulling!"

Peering over the back of an oak pew in the Jerusalem United Methodist Church, Kristi Noel King keeps close to her father. Arthur King, a member of the governing board of the church, grows tobacco near Warrenton.

The Southwest Indian country, a province of Catholic missionaries since Fray Marcos de Niza's arrival in 1539, has become in the present century an open territory where Presbyterians, Seventh-day Adventists, Mormons, Pentecostalists, and others also maintain missions.

Seventh-day Adventists, for instance, operate a school and a 25-bed hospital and dental clinic at Monument Valley, Utah, on the Navajo Indian Reservation. The eight-grade school employs two teachers and an assistant. One white and two Navajo pastors minister to spiritual needs, but the medical and educational impact of the mission has been far greater than the evangelistic. In 20 years the missionaries have baptized only 150 Navajos; but they deliver 200 babies a year, treat 1,500 bed patients, and handle 15,000 outpatient visits.

A thousand miles east of Monument Valley another missionary, the Reverend John Finn, drives the winding, rolling roads of the Ozark Mountains in a red Mustang bearing the bumper plaque, "Smile, God Loves You."

Brother John, as he is known to several thousand Southern Baptists in the four-county area he serves, is superintendent of missions with an office in Harrison, Arkansas. He coordinates the affairs of 32 churches, assists in finding new ministers when necessary, preaches on invitation, conducts revivals, leads vacation Bible schools, and knocks on doors to win people for Christ.

When I first met Brother John he was filling in for the pastor of the First Baptist Church of Lead Hill, Arkansas. His beliefs and his style are rooted deep in the fundamentalism of the southern Bible belt, and he is a powerful preacher. Holding the Bible in one lightly freckled hand and jabbing at it with the index finger of the other, he bore down for half an hour on the demands of Christian fellowship. Then he finished: "May the wind be at your backs and the sun on your faces till we meet again."

As the service ended, several people stepped up to welcome me, and soon the balding, 45-year-old minister joined the group. He introduced me to his son, Rodney, 15, and punched him lightly on the shoulder. "You didn't go to sleep on me back there, did you, fellow?" Rodney allowed that he had. "Impossible!" I exclaimed involuntarily, and Brother John smiled.

That night we attended a service in Harrison, and again I felt the warm friendliness of the congregation: After the benediction a group heading for a drive-in restaurant urged me to come along. There, at the Dairy Queen south of town, members of Harrison's five Southern Baptist churches gather after services to socialize. The talk at our table centered mainly on the need for preachers.

"Good pastors are hard to come by," said Brother John. "There aren't too many of them around. Maybe you've heard of the Baptist minister who had car trouble and, hoping to save a bit on the bill, told the mechanic, 'Now you remember, I'm just a poor preacher.' And the mechanic replied, 'Oh, I won't forget that. I heard you last Sunday.' "

Revivals are among the oldest and most colorful religious activities of fundamentalist churches. Many congregations have at least one a year to help increase membership with converts and to renew the dedication of the faithful. Often an out-of-town preacher is brought in to provide additional inspiration.

I attended the opening of a week-long revival at the Mountain Home Eastside Baptist Church, where Brother John had accepted an invitation to speak outside his territory. For his text he took the story of the woman of Samaria who, when she realized the identity of Christ, put down her heavy waterpot and ran into town to proclaim His coming.

"If *you* have any sin that prevents you from proclaiming Christ and working for Him, then it's a waterpot, it's a burden, and you ought to throw it down," he urged as the organ music rose. "Come share the Saviour. Throw down your burden." As he finished the call to the altar, the congregation began to sing, slowly:

> I've wandered far away from God,
> Now I'm coming home.
> The paths of sin too long I've trod,
> Lord, I'm coming home.

That first night the revival produced no converts; four people came forward to kneel and pray, but none volunteered to speak, "and of course we don't push them," Brother John said. As I took my leave he seemed a bit subdued, yet optimistic about the rest of the week. "The Christian life is a hard life, friend," he reminded me as we shook hands. "It's easier to mingle and drift."

A few weeks later, on a warm, humid Sunday in Vermont, I met a recent convert who left no doubt he was happier than he had been before. "Two years ago I was nothing, worthless," said Cliff Valley, a young carpenter, as he smacked the fist of one hand into the palm of another outside the lone church in North Thetford. "Then I was down to Salem, New Hampshire, visiting a friend. We went to church, and there was an altar call. Right then and there I just accepted Christ, and became a new man."

A few minutes earlier we had been inside North Thetford's white clapboard church and Cliff, long sideburns framing his face, was conducting the worship service in the absence of the vacationing minister. I had come to New England, the cradle of several Christian denominations, to see how small churches there were coping with declining attendance and rising costs—problems affecting both rural and urban churches nationwide.

In New England, as elsewhere, a number of congregations no longer able to support a pastor have settled for lay preachers, or for pastors who serve several churches of their denomination in an arrangement commonly called a "yoked parish." But there are more ecumenical possibilities, suggested by a roadside sign in North Thetford: "Federated Church." Actually, I discovered, neither the problems nor most of the solutions are new, and in this case the historic precedent goes back a long time. Both Congregationalists and Methodists have been attending this church since they built it in 1860 as a "union church," in which the congregation listened to a Methodist preacher one Sunday and a Congregationalist the next. In 1913 the two denominational groups federated, "in order to support a minister and be more efficient in winning the community to Christ."

But apparently fund raising was always a challenge. One Sunday in the early years the 50 people in attendance yielded up an offering of 22 cents, and the minister pronounced this benediction: "May the good Lord guide, preserve, and bless these parsimonious men and women. I can't."

From the landing of the Pilgrims, the history of the nation's settlement has been marked by establishment of religious colonies where the church dominated daily life. Today, most remaining communities of this kind are found in the West; but those of the Amish are an exception. Clustered mainly in Pennsylvania, Ohio, Indiana, and Ontario, Canada, about 70,000 Old Order Amish cling to their religious life-style; predominantly farmers, they survive by separating themselves from the outside world by their plain dress and speech and simple way of life.

Numerous other religious groups, particularly in the 19th century, have experimented with variations of communal living. Many sects failed, but as long as their individual settlements flourished they afforded members the opportunity to concentrate community organizational, educational, and religious efforts toward achieving the goals they held in common. Some towns thus established remain, but the way of life has changed: Orderville, Utah, a Mormon town of 400 souls, is an example; although all but four of its residents belong to the Church of Jesus Christ of Latter-day Saints, the town's communal experiment has long since passed into history.

A century ago, 24 Mormon families living under what church president Brigham Young termed a United Order pioneered the community, about 250 miles south of Salt Lake City, and each family deeded all it owned to the *(Continued on page 192)*

The Amish: a simple, ordered life

Photographs and text by ROBERT W. MADDEN

On Sunday morning Simon Swartzentruber, 81, puts on his black wide-
brimmed hat, picks up his cane, and
slowly walks the half mile from his
farm to the Amish church near Gortner,
Maryland. A descendant of Swiss
Anabaptists, Mr. Swartzentruber belongs
to one of several hundred Old Order
Amish congregations in North America.
Each has its Ordnung, the usually
unwritten body of rules that governs all
aspects of daily life—including the way
neighbor Harvey Yoder (above) tills his
soil "for the glory of the Lord."

Late afternoon sunbeam invades John C. Yoder's barn as he milks; Ruth Yoder keeps the cow's tail from switching her father's face. A younger daughter, Rebecca (opposite), serves supper to the barn cats gathering expectantly near the milk strainer. Each week when the family churns and molds butter, at least four quarts of buttermilk remain for morning griddle cakes. The Amish emphasize a simple, ordered life and old-fashioned values, and avoid such "worldly things" as electricity. Under state health regulations, milk cannot qualify as grade A unless stored in mechanically refrigerated tanks; so John must sell to canned-milk processors for a lower price. But to the Yoders, money has far less importance than their understanding of how God would have them conduct their lives.

Saturday chores in the Yoder home in Pleasant Valley, Maryland, include re-
filling the kerosene lamps. From her mother, an Amish girl learns many skills—
such as sewing, above—that she will need in running a household. As she
grows older, her parents encourage her in a broad range of duties so that she
will eventually become an accomplished wife and mother: the epitome of Amish
womanhood. For projects such as quilting, neighbors often combine efforts.

Using a gasoline-heated iron, Ruth Yoder presses one of the plain garments
typical of Amish styles; flatirons heat on the coal- and wood-burning cookstove.
The kitchen, sparkling clean and fragrant with the odors of cooking and baking,

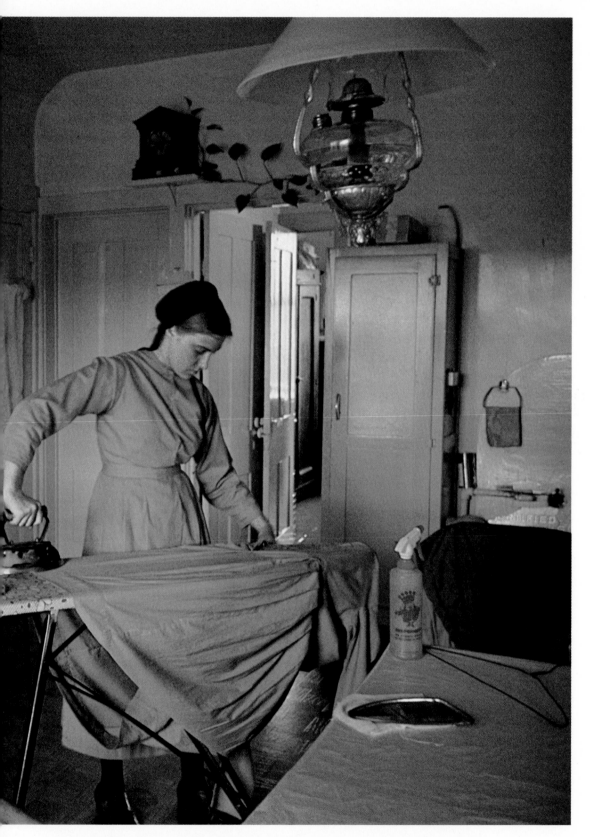

serves as the center of Amish home life and an inviting mealtime refuge on a chilly day. Here the womenfolk process most of the foods they serve, making egg noodles, preparing jams and jellies, canning fruits and vegetables.

With a mighty swing, the batter sends the ball
flying during a softball game at Swan Meadow,
an all-Amish school in western Maryland. More
than 70 children, including Albert Schrock
(opposite), attend the four-room public school
for grades one through eight. When in 1958 the
county condemned their one-room schoolhouse,
the Amish held a "school raising" and built
Swan Meadow rather than send their children
to a consolidated school in nearby Oakland. The
school grounds, four acres of rolling pastureland,
provide an ideal setting for a lunchtime picnic.

In a mechanical age, the Amish prefer to follow simple, old-time methods. John Yoder puts his buckwheat through a series of sieves to separate chaff from the grain. Sparks fly as Simon Swartzentruber repairs a buggy wheel at his forge. The Maryland Amish engage only in farming and a few related trades.

Under his father's watchful eye, Samuel Yoder helps string new barbed wire, a continuing chore on the Yoder farm. As they work side by side, John Yoder gives his son a practical education he knows school can never provide. Hence the formal education of an Amish child ends with the eighth grade. Above, Sam happily slices his cake for members of his family on his 16th birthday; now he shares in more responsibilities of the farm. Says his father, "He's going to be a farmer; we're going to have a father-son operation here. We're going to work!" The Amish thrive on hard work and frugality, and through farming they feel a spiritual affinity for the land and a sense of place in the community.

Homeward bound from church on a Sunday morning in May, buggies move

leisurely through Pleasant Valley. Old Order Amish do not own automobiles.

Unlike most Old Order Amish congregations, who hold their Sunday services in private homes, the Pleasant Valley folk have a meetinghouse. Here they gather every other Sunday for a three-hour service. In the austere interior, 60 families sing hymns reminiscent of some music of the 16th century. Colorful, state-required "slow-moving vehicle" signs relieve the solemn black of the buggies.

common good. Together they built houses, a dining hall, smithy, cooperage, tannery, shoe shop, furniture and woolen factories, lumber and grist mills. Soon they became all but self-sufficient.

Within a decade, however, a combination of factors—among them generally improved economic conditions, Brigham Young's death, and federal legislation outlawing plural marriage—led to the dissolution of what Professor Leonard J. Arrington, the official Latter-day Saints church historian, now describes as "an interesting social and economic experiment."

Today no evidence of those former industries exists in Orderville. I spent a hot afternoon drinking ice water and eating tart oxheart cherries with LeGrande C. Heaton, whose parents had lived under the United Order. The 73-year-old former mayor had picked the cherries himself by climbing into a towering tree.

"I didn't go to school, because my father was sick, you see," he told me, "and I had to help work the cattle. Stayed in the cattle business until 1924. That year, what with cars the coming thing, we built a gas station. I remember we sold ten gallons, in two five-gallon cans, for $9.80."

Today his station is one of the few businesses in the town; like the others, it is mostly dependent on summer tourists. Orderville's perpetual problem has been the departure of its young people. Mr. Heaton became clerk of the Orderville ward, or church district, in 1915, and held the position for 40 years. "During all that time," he said, "the birth rate here averaged 22 a year, and the death rate only two. But our population kept on sinking; and what with no real work here, there's still young people leaving now."

Yet almost all the young who travel the dirt road out of EskDale, Utah, about 150 miles northwest of Orderville, eventually return. And the more time I spent in this tightly-knit community of the Order of Aaron, the more I understood its appeal. "There are hardships here, and they bring us closer together," Douglas Childs told me. Doug, 41, lithe and tanned and as affable a man as I have ever met, was serving as spiritual leader of EskDale's 30 adults and 63 children—a job rotated among the community's several priests.

The late Maurice L. Glendenning, charismatic founder of the order, claimed to be descended from Aaron, brother of Moses and one of Israel's priestly tribe of Levi. Mr. Glendenning believed the Lord had called him to re-establish the ancient priesthood and prepare a refuge until the return of Christ to earth. In 1955 he organized EskDale as that refuge; here Aaronites may gather and purify themselves while they wait, explained his successor as chief high priest, Dr. Robert Conrad.

I first visited EskDale in the high desert heat of July. The poplar, Chinese elm, and Russian olive trees planted as windbreaks provided scant shade for the neat houses ringing the bare dirt compound. I was just in time for supper. Although the families live separately, they dine communally in a low-ceilinged hall. Work manager Stan Faber read a passage from the Bible, led a full-voiced rendition of "In the Sweet By and By," and ended with an extemporaneous prayer. Everyone ate in silence, but children as well as adults smiled at me and nodded. The women and girls wore blue jumpers over white blouses. Most men favored work pants and dark blue shirts with *Aaron* or *Levi* embroidered over the heart.

Next morning, after a breakfast of oatmeal, honey, cornbread, and applesauce, everyone older than 7 or 8 went to work: some to help bottle a truckload of cherries that had just arrived from Provo, others to lay the foundation for a new building, others to tend the garden, the grainfields, the beef and dairy cattle, the chickens, the honeybees.

On its 4,000 acres of brush-tufted desert the community strives for economic self-sufficiency. Any money an individual earns goes into the common fund. "We believe that one of the requirements of a true disciple of God is that you own no property," said Doug's wife, Karma, a gracious, contemplative woman with long sand-gold hair.

The Sabbath is observed on Saturday, when members of the order devote as much as eight hours to worship and Bible study.

There is also great emphasis on music; the 43-piece orchestra includes almost half of EskDale's population.

Motto of the Order of Aaron is "Education Unlimited!" Members teach all classes, from Montessori preschool through high school. The elementary school is part of the Millard County system; teachers' salaries go to the community. The children of ranchers, miners, and others in the vicinity can attend if their parents are willing to send them to school Sunday through Thursday.

The high school, with 30 students and nine unpaid teachers, operates on a $3,000 annual budget. "Our facilities are very humble, but we have a good product," Doug said. Of six graduates in 1973, five won college scholarships in agriculture, law, music, science, and nursing. One of the graduates of the late 1960's plans to return to EskDale as a doctor, and another as a veterinarian.

Some of the same pioneer qualities that have sustained the people of EskDale also characterize Frank Urick, whose ranch I visited in Montana. A man of strong emotions and determination, Frank champions the simple life his family leads in the foothills of the Highwood Mountains.

"I believe in rural living, and I want my kids to believe in it as I do," he said, tugging at his dark mustache. He, his wife, Vivian, and their seven children run 70 head of Hereford cattle on a thousand acres of rugged rangeland. Frank also works part time as a meatcutter at his sister Helen's locker plant in Belt, 13 miles away by gravel road. Sometimes Vivian works there, too.

Devout Catholics, the Uricks make the trip to church in Belt every Sunday except when snows block the road.

Despite the distances between ranches, they often get together with friends at rollicking dances in the barn Frank's neighbors helped him build, or at skating parties on a pond near the house.

The Uricks' oldest children balance ranch work with other

One of the spiritual leaders of the Order of Aaron, Douglas Childs serves as chief priest at EskDale, a Utah desert community founded by the group in 1955. Childs has nearly 50 piano students, teaches other musical instruments, and conducts the orchestra and band. Other EskDale residents work as farmers, carpenters, mechanics, teachers—and all take part daily in prayer, song, and Bible study.

interests: Jim, 21, and Dave, 19, ride bulls on the rodeo circuit; Lori, 17, and Pat, 16, are active students at Belt Valley High School.

As Frank and I talked over a fence rail one chill fall morning, his three youngest—Francie, 13, Joe, 12, and Matt, 9,—vaulted astride their Shetland ponies and clattered down the rock-strewn road toward Mountain Valley School, where they are the only students.

Mountain Valley is one of the rapidly diminishing number of one-room country schools—that favorite subject of American nostalgia. At the end of World War II the nation had more than 85,000 such schools; today, perhaps a thousand remain open. Yet educating their children at Mountain Valley is a tradition the Uricks very much want to keep. All the Urick children have attended the school, as did their father in the 1930's. "It's more leisurely here, and the kids can be a part of nature instead of just traveling through it on a bus," Frank said. "Sure, they don't get to mingle with other children, but they can catch up on that later."

When the youngsters finish their two-mile ride and turn the ponies out in the schoolyard to graze, their teacher, Sister Pauline Marn, greets them with a warm smile from the doorway of the white frame building. A Belt rancher's daughter with master's degrees in religion and education, Sister Pauline has been a Catholic Sister of Providence for 41 years. The trim, copper-haired nun spent 35 of those years teaching at parochial schools in Chicago and other cities. Two years ago she decided she wanted to come home. Now her life revolves around Mountain Valley, where she fulfills a nonsectarian teaching contract with the Cascade County school system.

On the first day I visited the school, the children worked through the morning to individual schedules, while Sister Pauline moved her own small chair from desk to desk, illustrating, questioning, explaining, correcting. At lunchtime the five of us ate our sandwiches and oranges in the classroom and then the children bolted for the door, free for half an hour.

Carpenter on weekdays, Cliff Valley of Lyme Center, New Hampshire, sometimes preaches on Sunday. He became a believer at a revival meeting in 1972, attended his hometown Baptist church for a while, then joined the Federated Church across the Connecticut River in North Thetford, Vermont, where he worships with Methodists and Congregationalists. Denominational distinctions have little significance for Cliff, who says, "It's all the one church of Christ."

Matt had discovered my interest in fossils, and shortly before the deadline he returned with thin sheets of shale, still moist, bearing imprints of shells and plants. The next day we pushed through the woods to Little Belt Creek, where Francie picked spearmint leaves for me to chew, and I repaid Matt's favor by finding him a frog.

There are obvious limitations to a tiny country school like Mountain Valley, but the Urick children enjoy at least two priceless benefits: relative freedom, and individual attention from a dedicated teacher. As I drove away from the ranch later I thought about my own children, and I suspected they might envy Matt and Francie and Joe.

I turned on the car radio. It was Sunday afternoon, and through the speaker came the words of a familiar old hymn:

> *Blest be the tie that binds*
> *Our hearts in Christian love.*
> *The fellowship of kindred minds*
> *Is like to that above.*

"The fellowship of kindred minds . . ." The phrase seemed to summarize the purpose and the strength not only of the churches but also the schools and other community organizations whose contribution to rural life had been my special preoccupation these recent months.

At the crest of a rise I stopped to look out across the Highwood Mountains, and then I realized what I would miss most when I left rural America, even more than the friends I had made: the peace that comes from open space and from solitude, a gift that the city by its very nature cannot provide. Perhaps it accounts for much of the patience, quiet wisdom, and sense of continuity we so often associate with rural folk. For me, it always will be reason enough to return.

The scholars
of Mountain Valley

PHOTOGRAPHS BY NICHOLAS deVORE III

*Walking the fence outside their one-room school
near Belt, Montana, surefooted Joe Urick sets the
pace for his sister Francie and brother Matt:
"I can do anything a chipmunk can, except crawl
into its hole." Matt prepares to raise the flag
as his teacher, Catholic Sister Pauline Marn,
talks with his father, Frank. After lunch, the
youngsters sit absorbed in an adventure story.*

Carefully avoiding the long, sharp spines of berry-laden hawthorns, Francie Urick moves through a stand of aspen trees near her school. She has spent the noon recess gathering plants —pale mauve mountain asters, a thick stalk of umbel, yellowing sprigs of chokecherry, and wisps of timothy—and will dry some in a bouquet that will last through the coming winter. The Urick children, the only pupils at Mountain Valley School, pursue the same studies as do others their age. "But they can take advantage of the woods around them for much of their science and nature study," says Sister Pauline, a nonsectarian teacher in the Cascade County school system. Born on a ranch near the school, she returned after 35 years of city teaching and now lives in a small addition to the classroom. "I relish the beauty, peace, and serenity here," she says. Below, Joe and Francie, with a dog between them, laze after school in a wind-rippled pasture.

Gathered around a tractor, the Urick family takes a few moments from the job of
running a ranch. All the children share in the work; Frank Urick believes their
education should include learning to ranch for a living. Jim and Dave, the two
oldest sons, also earn money riding bulls in rodeos. Dave (opposite, above) makes
a catch during barnyard passing practice. On the shop wall behind him hang
parts for horse-drawn implements the family still uses. Diverting the attention
of one of his nine brood sows with a can of grain, Frank leans forward to inspect
piglets born two days earlier in the straw-filled wooden farrowing house.

Wrangling horses in an open pasture beneath Rocky Butte, the youngest

Uricks and their dogs point the herd toward the corral half a mile away.

Index

Boldface indicates illustrations; *italic* refers to picture captions

Acknowledgments

The Special Publications Division is grateful to the individuals, organizations, and agencies named or quoted in the text and to those cited here for their generous cooperation and assistance during the preparation of this book: consultants at the U. S. Department of Agriculture, the U. S. Bureau of the Census, and the Smithsonian Institution; representatives of the Cooperative Extension Service in many states; and Ovid Bay, John Fetterman, John A. Hostetler, and Tom Hoy.

Additional Reading

The reader may want to check the *National Geographic Index* for related articles, and to refer to the Special Publication *American Mountain People* and to the following other books:

Sydney E. Ahlstrom, *A Religious History of the American People;* Rex R. Campbell, editor, *Beyond the Suburbs: The Changing Rural Life;* Foster Rhea Dulles, *A History of Recreation: America Learns to Play;* Federal Writers' Project, *American Guide Series* (state guidebooks); John A. Hostetler, *Amish Society;* Jay B. Nash, *Philosophy of Recreation and Leisure;* the National Academy of Sciences, *The Quality of Rural Living;* Fred A. Shannon, *The Farmer's Last Frontier;* Lewis R. Tamblyn, *Rural Education in the United States;* U. S. Department of Agriculture, *Contours of Change, the Yearbook of Agriculture for 1970.*

Library of Congress ⓒⓘⓟ Data
Main entry under title:
Life in rural America.
  A collection of essays by various
authors.
  1. United States—Social life and
customs—1945- 2. United States—
Rural conditions.
I. National Geographic Society,
Washington, D. C., Special Publica-
tions Division.
E169.02.L43   917.3'03'92   74-1562
ISBN 0-87044-146-9

Composition for *Life in Rural America* by National Geographic's Phototypographic
Division, Carl M. Shrader, Chief; Lawrence F. Ludwig, Assistant Chief. Printed and
bound by Fawcett Printing Corp., Rockville, Md. Color separations by Colorgraphics,
Inc., Beltsville, Md.; Graphic Color Plate, Inc., Stamford, Conn.; Progressive Color
Corp., Rockville, Md.; and J. Wm. Reed Co., Alexandria, Va.